# ISSUE FOCUSED FORENSIC
# CHILD CUSTODY ASSESSMENT

**Eric G. Mart, PhD, ABPP (Forensic)**

Highland Psychological Services
Manchester, New Hampshire

Professional Resource Press
Sarasota, Florida

*Published by*
Professional Resource Press
(An imprint of Professional Resource Exchange, Inc.)
Post Office Box 15560
Sarasota, FL 34277-1560

Printed in the United States of America

Copyright © 2007
by Professional Resource Exchange, Inc.

This publication is sold with the understanding that the publisher is not engaged in rendering professional services. If legal, psychological, medical, accounting, or other expert advice or assistance is sought or required, the reader should seek the services of a competent professional.

The copy editor for this book was Patricia Rockwood, the managing editor was Debbie Fink, the production coordinator was Laurie Girsch, and the typesetter was Richard Sullivan.

**Library of Congress Cataloging-in-Publication Data**

Mart, Eric G.
  Issue focused forensic child custody assessment / Eric G. Mart.
      p. cm. -- (Practitioner's resource series)
  Includes bibliographical references.
  ISBN 1-56887-111-2 (978-1-56887-111-0 : alk. paper)
  1. Custody of children--United States. 2. Family assessment--United States. 3. Forensic psychology--United States. I. Title.
  KF547.M367 2007
  346.7301'73--dc22
                              2007010932

# <u>DEDICATION</u>

*To my wife Kay
and my son Jonathan*

# SERIES PREFACE

As a publisher of books, multimedia materials, and continuing education programs, the Professional Resource Press strives to provide clinical and forensic professionals with highly applied resources that can be used to enhance skills and expand practical knowledge.

All of the titles in the Practitioner's Resource Series are designed to provide important new information on topics of vital concern to psychologists, clinical social workers, counselors, psychiatrists, and other clinical and forensic professionals.

Although the focus and content of each title in this series will be quite different, there will be notable similarities:

1. Each title in the series will address a timely topic of critical importance.
2. The target audience for each title will be practicing professionals. Our authors were chosen for their ability to provide concrete "how-to-do-it" guidance to colleagues who are trying to increase their competence in dealing with complex problems.
3. The information provided in these titles will represent "state-of-the-art" information and techniques derived from both experience and empirical research. Each of these guidebooks will include references and resources for those who wish to pursue more advanced study of the discussed topics.
4. The authors will provide case studies, specific recommendations, and the types of "nitty-gritty" details that practitioners need before they can incorporate new concepts and procedures into their offices.

We feel that one of the unique assets of Professional Resource Press is that all of our editorial decisions are made by practitioners. The publisher, all editorial consultants, and all reviewers are practitioners and academic scientist-practitioners.

If there are other topics you would like to see addressed in this series, please let me know.

*Lawrence G. Ritt, Publisher*

# ABSTRACT

This book is designed to present a focused, issue-oriented approach to child custody assessment. Common models of custody assessment will be briefly described, and the strengths and weaknesses of each will be examined, from both a clinical/forensic and an ethical perspective. The movement toward more focused custody assessments will be outlined and the literature on this trend briefly discussed. The rationale of the issue focused forensic approach will be presented, and a step-by-step guide to conducting such assessments will be provided.

# TABLE OF CONTENTS

**THE ISSUE FOCUSED FORENSIC CHILD CUSTODY ASSESSMENT: PRACTICAL APPLICATION** *(Continued)*

# ISSUE FOCUSED FORENSIC CHILD CUSTODY ASSESSMENT

## CHILD CUSTODY ASSESSMENTS – CONTEXT AND HISTORY

Child custody assessment is an increasingly complex and contentious area of forensic practice. There are many reasons why custody assessment is so challenging for psychologists. This section of the book will outline some of the inherent difficulties in performing such assessments.

One of the obvious problems that arises in performing custody evaluations concerns the ill-defined nature of the task. In many other areas of forensic practice, the parameters of particular types of assessments are far less ambiguous. To give an example by way of contrast, one well-established area of forensic practice is the assessment of competence to stand trial. Although the legal statutes that govern the determination of competence vary from state to state, in general the standard is based on the parameters laid out in the case of Dusky (*Dusky v. United States*, 1960). The *Dusky* standard states that in order to be considered competent to stand trial, a defendant must have a reasonable factual and rational grasp of the charges and the nature of the proceedings, as well as the ability to consult with his or her attorney with a reasonable degree of factual and rational understanding. In some jurisdictions, there is an additional requirement that any deficits in rational and factual grasp of the issues involved in standing trial must be related to a mental disease or defect, such as a thought disorder, mental retardation, or brain damage. *Factual* in this context relates to, among other things, a knowledge of the nature of the charges, the roles of the participants, the adversarial nature of the proceedings, and the strength of the evidence against the defendant. *Rational* relates to the idea that the defendant's thought processes regarding the proceedings are not overly affected by delusions or other disordered thought processes.

Although performing high quality competency assessments requires training and skill, the issues are fairly straightforward. The job of the evaluator is to provide expert information to the court regarding the defendant's understanding of the issues related to standing trial and the underlying cause of any observed deficits. Grisso (2003) has provided an evaluation model for the assessment of competence to stand trial which has been very influential in this area of practice as well as in the assessment of other psycholegal issues. His five-step methodology proceeds as follows:

1. *Functional Component:* In this part of the assessment, the evaluator directly assesses the defendant's understanding of the important issues involved in standing trial. Structured interviews and instruments such as the MacArthur Competence Assessment Tool-Criminal Adjudication (MacCAT-CA; Hoge et al., 1999), Georgia Court Competency Test (GCCT; Wildman et al., 1978), Competency to Stand Trial Assessment Instrument (CAI; Laboratory of Community Psychiatry, Harvard Medical School, 1973), and Competence Assessment for Standing Trial for Defendants With Mental Retardation (CAST-MR; Everington, 1992) are available to assist in data collection. If no deficits are observed, the assessment stops. If deficits are observed, the evaluation moves on to the Causal component.

2. *Causal:* In this step of the assessment, the evaluator seeks to explain the cause of any observed deficits. This may involve IQ testing to assess the possibility of mental retardation, mental status examination, clinical interviews, record review, and personality testing to determine whether a psychiatric condition may play a role in observed deficits. Malingering or other forms of impression management may also be assessed.

3. *Person-Situation Congruence:* In this component of the evaluation, the defendant's strengths and weaknesses are considered in context. For example, a mildly retarded adolescent may be able to cope with a trial on charges of simple assault stemming from an incident in which he pushed a teacher,

but may have much more trouble with a drug sales case in which there are multiple defendants, complicated issues of law related to the legality of a search, and a need for the defendant to testify.

4. *Conclusory:* In this component of the assessment, the evaluator gives his or her opinion regarding the ultimate issue (the legal issue being decided, in this case competence). There is some controversy regarding the propriety of offering such a conclusion; some feel that the ultimate issue is a legal question and not the province of the evaluator, and others feel that the expert should provide an opinion and allow the court to give it whatever weight is deemed appropriate.

5. *Remediative:* In this part of the assessment, the evaluator may provide an opinion about whether any observed deficits are amenable to therapy, medications, or other interventions that might restore the defendant to competence.

In competency assessments, this model can be applied to the psycholegal issue (whether the defendant meets the *Dusky* standard) in a straightforward manner in order to assist the court in its determination. The evaluation of competence has reasonably clear parameters, evaluative methodologies that have wide acceptance, and psychological instruments that have a clear relationship to the issues being assessed. Unfortunately, this is not the case in custody assessment, and this state of affairs exists for a number of reasons. In order to understand why this is the case, a brief review of child custody and custody assessments will be helpful.

## THE TENDER YEARS MODEL

It must be understood that the idea that there might be a dispute between parents over the custody of their children is a fairly recent development. For most of recorded history, children have been considered the chattel property of their fathers. This is not surprising, because it has only been in the latter half of the 20th century that adult women have had equal legal rights with men, and then only in Westernized cultures. However, in the United States and Britain, around the early 1900s, the *tender years* doctrine began to be recognized. This doctrine initially arose out of a developing attitude that there was something intrinsically wrong and improper about removing a nursing infant from his or her mother's breast. This later gradually expanded to include more than the act of nursing, beginning to reflect a societal assumption that the best place for young children was in the care of their mother. However, children were expected to be returned to the control of their fathers once they were older and more self-sufficient. Ultimately, in the United States the tender years doctrine was expanded to include the assumption that, in cases of divorce, there was what amounted to a rebuttable assumption that children should be raised by their mothers, and fathers should be relegated to visitation and child support.

## THE LEAST DETRIMENTAL ALTERNATIVE MODEL

The presumptions of the tender years doctrine were bolstered by the work of Goldstein, Freud, and Solnit in their seminal work *Beyond the Best Interests of the Child* (1979), which had an enormous influence on child protection and social service agencies and the law in relation to child custody proceedings. The model of child custody that emerged from this book was referred to as "the least detrimental alternative" because it was designed to make the best of an already bad situation, that is, a divorce. A central idea in this treatise is that divorce and child dependency courts should give considerable priority to protecting the relationship between the child and his or her primary attachment figure, which Goldstein et al. termed the psychological parent. This conceptualization of the psychological parent is different from the term "attachment," which is also utilized in child custody matters. Goldstein et al.'s conceptualization of the psychological parent is more black and white. They suggest that although children can have multiple attachments with varying degrees of emotional connection, there are no degrees of intensity and only one psychological parent. In addition, Goldstein et al. argue that there will be dire consequences if the bond between the child and the psychological parent is broken by even short interruptions or placement outside the family home. They suggest that irreparable damage can occur to children 2 years old or younger in a matter of a few days of separation, although this interval could be extended as the child matures. Goldstein et al. also made it clear that in cases where young children are placed with surrogate parents for periods approaching a year, these caretakers should automatically be considered the psychological parents.

Because most families in the latter half of the 20th century consisted of a father who worked outside the home and a mother who worked in the home, ran the household, and took primary responsibility for rearing the family's children, it was natural for mental health professionals to assume that the mother was the psychological parent. It is easy to see how the tender years doctrine and the concept of the psychological parent combined to create a situation that strongly favored mothers receiving primary physical custody of the children in most contested divorces. Although a particular mother might be found to be unfit to be the primary custodian of the children, because of societal attitudes, assumptions of mental health professionals influenced by the concept of the psychological parent model, and the orientation of the courts, this was the exception rather than the rule. Custody evaluations by mental health professionals (which were less common in the past) were generally oriented toward ruling out such unfitness.

However, starting in the 1970s, women increasingly began to enter the workplace and pursue careers. Rather than following the traditional pattern in which the father was in the workplace and the mother was in the home, many families now were supported by the labor of both parents, and some of the responsibility for child rearing was transferred to day care centers and after-school programs. Although women continued to shoulder a disproportionate share of domestic duties, there was a move toward more egalitarian division of labor and child-rearing duties. Fathers began to have more contact with their younger children and to spend more time caring for them. At the same time, the idea of equal rights for women in the workplace and in all areas of society made sex-based presumptions about parenting less accepted and to some extent politically incorrect. In addition, research began to demonstrate that children reared in a variety of different custody arrangements (primary mother, primary father, joint physical, etc.) showed no robust differences in their adjustment or long-term outcomes. This led to a new phase in child custody determination and assessment. Courts began to adopt "sex blind" policies toward child custody. Both parents could now come before the court and ask to be judged on their individual merits as parents, and the more expedient assumptions of the tender years doctrine were abandoned. This new set of circumstances required mental health professionals to perform more comprehensive and nuanced assessments of the family, encompassing a much wider set of issues.

## THE PRIMARY CARETAKER MODEL

In more recent years, another model has been increasingly utilized by the courts in making custody determinations. This has been commonly referred to as the primary caretaker model. This model examines the roles of both parents in the lives of their children and gives preference for custody to the parent who has performed the bulk of the child care activities. This greatly simplifies the process of deciding custody because it relies on criteria that, for the most part, can be easily quantified. A guardian ad litem or mental health professional can check pediatric records to see which parent usually brings the child for medical appointments, does drop-offs and pick-ups at school, attends parent teacher conferences, and so forth. Obviously, those utilizing this model still look at the nature of the relationship between the parents and children, as well as issues such as child abuse and domestic violence. But, all things being equal, preference is given to the parent who has provided more day-to-day child care.

A problem with this model is that it assumes that the parent who has provided most of the child care up to the point of the divorce would necessarily be the better parent postdivorce. This assumption may not be true. For example,* a given family may organize child care and breadwinner roles along traditional lines: The father may work long hours to support the family while the mother stays home with the children. The primary caretaker model assumes that the mother should be considered the better parent. However, it may well be the case that the father is much more skilled in dealing with the children and would perform better in the role of primary caretaker than the mother.

It must be understood that these three models of custody are generally not clearly or officially articulated in the legal statutes governing custody, but are utilized rather as general guidelines for the determination of the best interest of children by the courts having jurisdiction. In addition, as applied in the real world, these views of custody are not mutually exclusive. A judge or marital master might give great weight to determining which parent is the psychological parent, or might subscribe more to a multiple attachment view of the issue of attachment and bonding. At the same time, the judge's opinion about the importance of the bond may be tempered by pragmatic

---

* Names and identifying characteristics in all case examples have been changed to protect confidentiality.

considerations. For example, a couple's children may have been placed in the temporary custody of one parent during the pendency of the divorce, and the judge may decide to leave well enough alone if the children are functioning reasonably well under this arrangement. Another judge may simply hold a traditional view of family life and believe that young children should spend the bulk of their time with their mother absent serious problems with that parent. Regardless, these three views of child custody are the most prevalent and form the context in which the psychologist's custody evaluation takes place.

## CHILD CUSTODY ASSESSMENT GUIDELINES AND MODELS

The mental health professional's role as expert to the court is to provide information that is not readily known or understood, using his or her experience, structured interviews, record review, and diagnostic tests to assist in the decision-making process. The expert's testimony is generally related to a particular psycholegal question or construct. In the case of competence to stand trial, the issue is the defendant's factual and rational understanding of the proceedings and ability to consult with his or her attorney. In MSTO (mental state at time of offense, also known as not guilty by reason of insanity) the issue turns on the defendant's understanding of the wrongfulness of his or her actions, ability to control his or her actions, and the presence or absence of a pathological cause for any observed deficits. In evaluations regarding an individual's ability to make a valid will (testamentary capacity) the issue concerns the individual's knowledge that he or she is making a will, knowledge of his or her assets, understanding of the persons to whom one would normally want to leave one's property, and ability to hold all of these issues in mind while executing the will. A psychologist assessing testamentary capacity would be guided by these legal criteria and would provide information to the court about the testator's knowledge of the issues listed above, as well as the reasons for any observed deficits (dementia, depression, psychosis, etc.). It is easy to see how Grisso's (2003) five-step model of evaluation would be helpful in these types of assessments, because the psycholegal issues are reasonably well defined and circumscribed.

But the issue is not nearly so clear when we consider the practice of child custody assessment, in large part because of the way in which the psycholegal issues are framed. In custody assessments, the term "best interests of the child" is offered in the statutes of many jurisdictions as the guiding principle for determining the best child custody arrangements. In response to the legal system's use of this term in framing the psycholegal issues in these types of assessments, a number of organizations have developed guidelines specifically related to custody evaluations, such as the American Psychological Association (APA) "Guidelines for Child Custody Evaluations in Divorce Proceedings" (American Psychological Association, 1994) and the Association of Family and Conciliation Courts "AFCC Model Standards of Practice for Child Custody Evaluation" (Association of Family and Conciliation Courts, May 2006). Both organizations appear to take the position that the purpose of custody evaluations is to provide information to the courts about the best interests of the child or children involved in the divorce. The APA "Guidelines for Child Custody Evaluations in Divorce Proceedings" explicitly delineate the purpose of custody evaluations as follows:

1. The primary purpose of the evaluation is to assess the best psychological interests of the child.
2. The child's interests and well-being are paramount.
3. The focus of the evaluation is on parenting capacity, the psychological and developmental needs of the child, and resulting fit.

The stated purpose of the custody evaluations as outlined above is problematic. A growing number of authors have raised concerns about the extent to which issues such as "best interests of the child" (BIC) and "fit" can be reliably and validly measured. The current state of research available on this subject offers little guidance regarding the relationship between parent variables, child variables, custody arrangements, and visitation schedules and outcomes for the children involved. This has led some prominent authors to question the basis for clinicians' conclusions in child custody assessments. O'Donohue and Bradley (1999) suggest that custody evaluations as currently undertaken are based as much on the unstated value judgments of psychologists as on science, and that the current state of the science in this field does not allow empirically defensible conclusions to be drawn with any degree of scientific certainty. Others, such as Grisso (2003), have raised similar concerns about both the scientific underpinnings of custody evaluations and the methods used specifically in such assessments. In an attempt to clarify these issues and offer guidance for legal and mental health professionals charged with assisting courts in determining BIC, the laws of many states outline areas to be considered in determining BIC. Unfortunately, these statutes often raise more issues than they resolve. As an example, Michigan's standards for custody decisions, which have been very influential throughout the country, dictate that child custody decisions by the courts take into account the following:

1. The love, affection, and other emotional ties existing between the competing parties and the child.
2. The capacity and disposition of competing parties to give the child love, affection, and guidance and continuation of educating and raising the child in its religion or creed, if any.
3. The capacity and disposition of competing parties to provide the child with food, clothing, medical care, or other remedial care recognized and permitted under the laws of the state in lieu of medical care and other material needs.
4. The length of time the child has lived in a stable, satisfactory environment and desirability of maintaining continuity.
5. The permanence as a family unit of the existing or proposed custodial home.
6. The moral fitness of the competing parties.
7. The mental and physical health of the competing parties.
8. The home, school, and community records of the child.
9. The reasonable preference of the child, if the court deems the child to be of sufficient age to express preference.
10. Any other factor considered by the court to be relevant to a particular child custody dispute.

All of these factors have face validity, and it would be difficult to imagine how a reasonable decision about child custody could be made without considering some or all of these factors. But as Grisso (2003) points out, these factors are difficult to measure with any degree of precision. In addition, it is not clear what weight should be given to each factor in relation to the others, and the court has broad discretion in determining which of these factors to consider and how to prioritize them. Consequently, any attempt to derive a reliable methodology for determining BIC based on these factors is likely to be inadequate. In the same way, the general idea behind an attempt to assess fit between the particular strengths, weaknesses, and psychological adjustment of a particular parent and similar factors in a child can involve a large number of ill-defined and dynamic variables. Because there is no scientific method of determining the relationship between these variables and a concept as nebulous as fit, the most likely outcome of any attempt to assess such an issue will be a melange of scientific data, clinical judgment, and personal opinions. Further, the relationship between the information elicited and relied on and the conclusions rendered is likely to remain obscure.

## THE BEST INTERESTS STANDARD

One of the major issues that contribute to this unfortunate state of affairs in performing custody assessments may be related to the way in which the purpose of such evaluations is formulated. As previously noted, in most other areas of forensic psychology, the purpose of an evaluation is much more technical and circumscribed than in custody assessments. The assessment of an individual's competence to stand trial is generally quite focused and closely informed by the controlling statute in the jurisdiction in which the evaluation is performed. As previously mentioned, the APA "Guidelines for Child Custody Evaluations in Divorce Proceedings" states: "The primary purpose of evaluation is to assess the best psychological interests of the child. . . . The child's best interests and well being are paramount" (p. 677). Perhaps even more problematic, under the heading "Procedural Guidelines: Conducting a Child Custody Evaluation" it is stated that "The scope of the evaluation is determined by the evaluator, based on the nature of the referral question" (p. 678). These guidelines define the role of the psychologist in custody assessments in much more broad and vague terms than is the case in any other area of forensic practice. For example, the role of the psychologist in performing an NGRI (not guilty by reason of insanity) assessment is not defined in professional guidelines as "supporting the American system of jurisprudence." Forensic psychologists define their roles much more narrowly in other types of evaluations. The APA custody guidelines are characterized by O'Donohue and Bradley as "vague, quite general, and do not indicate specific practices or techniques to be used in evaluations" (pp. 316-317). They rightly suggest that these guidelines are actually a collection of ethical standards and are "largely truisms" (O'Donohue & Bradley, 1999). This pervasive lack of focus and rigor contributes to the likelihood that psychologists will overreach in custody assessments and usurp the role of the fact finder.

The problem of assessing BIC is further complicated by the lack of longitudinal research regarding the outcomes of various custody and visitation arrangements. Those studies that have been done have not demonstrated robust effects for any particular arrangement, even when factors such as conflict level between parents are considered, and the results of studies run in different directions. There is research that suggests that more extreme maladaptive behaviors on the part of parents, either individually or as a dyad, contribute to poorer outcomes. However, findings that indicate that child exposure to ongoing high conflict between divorced parents and witnessing or being the victim of domestic violence lead to poorer outcomes, though important, are hardly counterintuitive.

## PREVAILING METHODOLOGIES, INSTRUMENTS, AND TECHNIQUES

Problems also exist concerning the methods used by psychologists in performing custody evaluations. Many mental health professionals use no explicit methodology for custody evaluations, but instead rely heavily on experience and clinical judgment. This approach runs counter to a formidable body of scientific literature, which indicates that clinical judgment is often unreliable and that experience does not necessarily add validity to a clinician's conclusions (Dawes, Faust, & Meehl, 1989). Nevertheless, those evaluators who rely on clinical judgment are not necessarily less accurate in their conclusions than those who use the various methodologies that have been developed for conducting custody evaluations. This is because most of the prevailing methodologies either lack empirical support or are predicated on explicit theories that have not been empirically tested, such as family systems or psychodynamic personality theory. Many of these theories, although they may have some utility in a clinical setting, cannot be falsified or empirically tested. In *Daubert v. Merrell Dow Pharmaceuticals, Inc.* (1993), the United States Supreme Court specifically referenced Karl Popper's (1992) citation of psychoanalytic theory as an unscientific theory because its assumptions could not be empirically tested. And, although the five-point test outlined in *Daubert* for determining whether expert testimony is scientific and thus admissible has been very influential in criminal proceedings, it does not appear to have exerted much influence on custody evaluators.

Further, not only are many child custody evaluation methodologies based on shaky or nonexistent theoretical foundations, but many of the evaluation techniques that they employ are seriously flawed. In their 1996 article, Michaela Heinze and Thomas Grisso (1996) reviewed a number of the commonly used custody assessment instruments in terms of their psychometric properties. According to their analysis, many of the instruments that are used frequently by mental health professionals have serious psychometric flaws, including low reliability and very questionable validity. Although the issue of the specific utility of custody related psychometric tests will be examined in greater detail in a later section of this book, it is helpful to use an example of how many widely accepted and utilized custody assessment methods are employed without established reliability and validity. The practice of observing parent and child interactions either in the home or office, for example, is recommended by many psychology texts and articles (Schutz et al., 1989). M. J. Ackerman and M. C. Ackerman (1997) surveyed 201 psychologists around the United States with regard to child custody evaluation practices. They found that a high percentage of the psychologists included observations of parent-child interactions as a component of their evaluations. Different authors suggest differing methods for conducting parent/child observations. The Uniform Child Custody Evaluation System developed by Munsinger and Karlson (1994) is fairly typical in suggesting that the evaluator observe parent and child in a free play situation and then have the parent and child engage in a structured problem-solving situation such as assembling a puzzle or playing checkers. Clearly, it makes sense that a psychologist who bases custody and visitation recommendations at least in part on the quality of parent-child interactions would include observations of these interactions in determining BIC. However, a review of the PsychInfo database found no research that compared conclusions derived from observations of parent-child interaction in custody assessments with outcomes for children involved. There is even evidence that the use of this general technique can lead to incorrect conclusions regarding the nature of a child's relationship with a parent or caretaker. Milchman (2000) has pointed out that evaluators doing such observations often confuse warm, friendly relationships with attachment and/or bonding. An evaluator may observe a stand-offish quality in a child's interactions with a parent whom the child has not seen in some time. A subsequent observation of the child having trouble separating from the parent at the end of the visit may lead the evaluator to conclude that this pattern of interaction reflects a dislike of the parent on the child's part. However, Milchman points out that well-bonded children who are separated from a parent may express anger upon reintroduction to the parent and may show distress at being again separated, and that it takes a good deal of investigation to determine the true state of affairs. It is of concern that an assessment technique so widely utilized in contributing to custody decisions by professionals should stand on what is, at best, extremely tenuous methodological ground. Similar problems exist with virtually all custody assessment techniques that attempt to determine BIC.

## THE ISSUE OF COMPREHENSIVENESS: CAN MORE BE LESS?

Many professional writers on the subject of custody evaluations call for far-reaching data collection, including record review, observations, home visits, and multiple interviews with family members, relatives, neighbors, and teachers. Partly as a result of this, the expense of custody evaluations, always high, has increased in recent years. A study by M. J. Ackerman and M. C. Ackerman (1997) surveying the custody evaluation practices of 201 experienced mental health professionals across the country found that the average cost of a custody evaluation was $2,645.96, and fees ranged as high as $15,000.00. This expense creates a situation in which custody evaluations are often out of the reach of divorcing parties, and information that might assist the court is not elicited due to the expense.

Further, more information is not necessarily better. Although many evaluators claim to rely on the totality of the data, a substantial body of research indicates that most, if not all, practitioners rely and base their conclusions on a few salient pieces of data (Garb, 1998). Although it is certainly important to gather and confirm relevant information when performing child custody evaluations, in practice there often appears to be no rationale for data collection and/or prioritization of issues to be explored. Evaluators may administer an extensive psychological assessment of all of the parties in a custody assessment, which might include (a) clinical interviews (either one or multiple interviews); (b) mental status examinations of the parents and/or the children; (c) more or less extensive psychometric and/or projective testing; and (d) reports from collateral sources, which may include interviews with or letters from extended family members, neighbors, family friends, teachers, day care providers, employers, and a variety of health care providers. There is no clear point at which the conscientious evaluator should stop collecting data. I was recently involved in a custody case in which a reputable psychologist produced a 108-page single-spaced custody report in addition to two other psychological testing reports that another psychologist had provided at the behest of the primary examiner. The bulk of the verbiage in this report was made up of the statements of collateral information sources. It should be noted that the family in question had only one preschool-aged child, and I can only wonder how long the report would have been if there had been five or six children. The type of free-wheeling data collection employed in this admittedly extreme example raises ethical issues above and beyond its impact on the validity of conclusions based on such data. The "Specialty Guidelines for Forensic Psychologists" (Committee on Ethical Guidelines for Forensic Psychologists, 1991) point out (VI, F. 2.): "With respect to evidence of any type, forensic psychologists avoid offering information from their investigations or evaluations that does not bear directly upon the purpose of their professional services and that is not critical as support for their product, evidence or testimony, except where such disclosure is required by law." Although this is not stated explicitly in this standard, it is implied (and explicitly stated in other portions of the Guidelines) that there must be respect for the privacy of those being evaluated, and that only information likely to bear directly on the legal issue at hand should be elicited from the client. Unfortunately, there are pressures that motivate psychologists to gather more and more information about families in custody evaluations. In this regard, Amundson et al. have stated: "Consequently, in their desire to be helpful, psychologists may, in their inquiry regarding 'children's best interests' conduct quasi experimental procedures, invade privacy, and induce patients to abandon constitutional rights in the service of obtaining 'good data' and evidence for the court" (Amundson, Daya, & Gill, 2000, p. 68).

The absence of an explicit methodology and rationale for data collection can create a situation in which custody evaluators collect information in ways that can be intrusive for families and children without adequate justification for this violation of privacy. In addition, parents sometimes reveal information that becomes part of the court record and has the effect of increasing emotional tensions and conflict. Certain things that are done and said in the heat of a custody battle cannot be undone or unsaid. An Arab proverb says, "There are cures for the wounds of lead and steel, but the wounds of the heart, they never heal." It is not clear how the risk of such intrusive data collection is counterbalanced against the need for comprehensive assessment, nor does it appear that this issue has been widely considered.

It is possible that continued research regarding custody assessment, custody and visitation arrangements, and outcomes for children may eventually improve the reliability and validity of comprehensive child custody assessments. In my opinion, the current state of the science in this area at the present time is not sufficiently developed to provide reliable and valid conclusions about the best interests of children who are before the court in custody matters. As previously noted, O'Donohue and Bradley (1999) and others have suggested that child custody evaluations in their present form are not reliable or valid enough to be given serious consideration by the courts. Following these conclusions, it would seem logical that psychologists should cease performing such evaluations and testifying about custody and visitation in divorces. It would also follow that the presentation of expert reports and testimony in custody matters by psychologists is counterproductive, in that rather than assisting the trier of fact by providing reliable technical information, custody assessments and testimony as presently practiced actually usurp the role of the court. As matters presently stand, psychologists are often substituting their personal preferences and judgments about lifestyles for scientific data. Although judges and guardians ad litem clearly make their decisions based in part on moral beliefs and personal preferences, they are empowered by our society to make such decisions, while psychologists, as experts to the court, are not.

Despite these problems, it appears unlikely that divorce courts will dispense with the services of psychologists and other mental health professionals in the foreseeable future. If anything, there appears to be an ongoing expansion of the role of mental health professionals in areas associated with child custody. This raises the question of whether it is possible to perform child custody evaluations in an ethical and scientifically defensible manner that is of assistance to the courts.

This issue has been addressed in a number of ways by mental health professionals. One important contribution has been made by Melton et al. (2007). Although these authors express serious concerns and reservations regarding mental health professionals' involvement in custody cases, they suggest that an ethically defensible role is that of investigator. In this role, the mental health professional assists the court by using his or her knowledge of child development and family functioning to provide the court with information about relationships within a particular family. Such information is gathered through interviews with children and parents in the family as well as data provided by diverse collateral sources. Melton et al. suggest that information gathered in this manner may provide the court with a framework for making determinations about the disposition of a particular custody case. Further, they suggest that the quality of this information may be superior to that provided by court-appointed guardians ad litem, assuming that the clinician has specialized experience working with families and children. This approach purposely sidesteps the problems of determining BIC by explicitly changing the role of the evaluator from arbiter of best interest to one who assists the court by providing information without impinging on the court's prerogatives. A sample report utilizing this model is provided on pages 67 to 74.

## THREE MODELS OF CUSTODY ASSESSMENT

When the literature on child custody assessment is reviewed, it becomes clear that there are three basic models utilized in performing such assessments. Although there is no clear consensus on the names of these models, for purposes of this discussion they can be labeled as follows:

1. The comprehensive model
2. The mini-evaluation model
3. The issue focused forensic model

A review of the literature suggests that the comprehensive model is the one most commonly employed by custody evaluators, and it is reflected in the guidelines of a number of influential professional organizations. As previously noted, this model directs evaluators to gather information comprehensively from a wide variety of sources. The APA "Guidelines for Child Custody Evaluations in Divorce Proceedings" are typical in recommending that evaluators, at minimum, utilize the following sources of data:

1. Interviews of each parent or caretaker, both alone and together
2. Interviews of each child
3. Psychological testing of the parents
4. Psychological testing of the children
5. Observations of the children interacting with the parents
6. Interviews with persons who may have knowledge of the parents and children
7. Review of records

As previously noted, the APA standards explicitly state that the scope of the evaluation is to be determined by the evaluator and that the guiding principle of this model of assessment is the best interests of the family's children. This model has a number of strengths and weaknesses. The most obvious weakness is that there is no scientific evidence that evaluations undertaken utilizing this model will arrive at valid conclusions regarding what kind of custody arrangement will produce the best outcome for the children. This is not surprising, because it would be difficult, if not impossible, to assess the reliability and validity of the conclusions drawn from comprehensive custody assessments. This is in part due to the fact that the very nature of this model makes comparison across subjects impossible. Utilizing the APA guidelines, the scope of the evaluation, use or nonuse of psychological testing, tests utilized, number and length of interviews with the family members, number and extent of collateral contacts, and the length and content of parent-child observations are explicitly left up to the evaluator. Consequently, although the APA guidelines provide a general approach to the issue of child custody assessment, they do not provide an explicit methodology.

For these reasons, there are probably as many approaches to performing comprehensive model assessments as there are clinicians performing them. This situation could be improved by the adoption of a set of specific items that would always be assessed, and some authors have offered their own protocols in this regard. Jonathan Gould's important book, *Conducting Scientifically Crafted Child Custody Evaluations* (2006), does a great deal to advance the practice of child custody evaluation by providing an explicit set of goals for assessment and then linking these goals to a specific evaluative methodology, with emphasis on providing maximum reliability and validity. I personally feel that Gould's rationale and suggested procedures offer much more than the APA custody guidelines, which supposedly govern this area of practice.

Clearly, when a comprehensive assessment is called for, adoption of such a protocol or structured approach greatly improves the quality of the evaluation. The use of a structured approach to custody assessment would have the same advantages that Rogers (1995) suggests in his advocacy for the use of structured interviews in the assessment of personality. A structured approach allows the clinician to standardize his or her approach to the interview portion of the assessment. Rather than asking questions and gathering information extemporaneously, the clinician approaches a particular domain related to diagnosis with similar queries every time he or she interviews a client. This allows for the comparison of a particular patient's responses to other patients questioned in the same manner. At the same time, the structured approach allows the interview to become a kind of psychometric instrument which lends itself to research and different types of scoring. The use of a structured instrument also allows for the development of norms, reliability, and validity scores. Although it is not a foregone conclusion that the use of a structured assessment methodology in custody assessment would increase validity, at minimum it would likely increase reliability. But, as previously mentioned, such structured and uniform approaches to this type of assessment are not generally employed, and a drawback to the use of the comprehensive methodology continues to be the lack of standardization.

Another evaluation methodology which has become better known in recent years is the mini-evaluation, or mini-eval. This model of assessment was developed in Los Angeles, where a combination of high levels of docket pressure on domestic relations courts and large numbers of child custody cases in which money was not available for comprehensive evaluation helped create this approach to assessment. It is questionable whether the mini-eval should really be considered a methodology at all; it is more of a general approach to fast-track evaluation of both general and specific issues in child custody cases before the court. Judges in these courts, requiring quick answers to pressing questions in divorces involving child custody, would refer matters to clinicians in the court clinics. These clinicians would utilize interviews to gather information about the referral question; psychometric testing was rarely utilized, either because of the time and expense involved or because clinicians in the court clinics were not qualified to administer it. Referral questions might concern the emotional status of the parents or children, attachment/relationship issues, domestic violence, alcohol and drug abuse, overnight visitation of infants and younger children, or any other issue about which the court required information. Additionally, more general issues, including the ultimate issue, could be addressed by these clinicians. As time went on, this model of assessment was also adopted by clinicians in private practice, and it is sometimes referred to as a fast-track assessment. In this model of assessment, the evaluating clinician gives his or her report to the court and is cross-examined, but no written report is produced.

The problems with this model are obvious. As with the comprehensive model, there are no specific standards regarding methods of data collection, nor is there any clear sense of how particular evaluators weigh the information they elicit. A review of the PsychInfo database failed to uncover a single article dealing with this model of assessment. The brief time allowed for the completion of the evaluation severely limits the ability of the evaluator to gather collateral data or otherwise confirm the information provided by the parties. This model also seems to indicate that a psychologist, social worker, or other mental health expert would be able to get to the truth of complex issues related to BIC through a few hours of interviewing and possibly a few phone calls. The emergence of this model is certainly understandable, in that courts are often required to make important decisions in custody disputes with little in the way of resources and data. It could be argued that some data is better than no data in the decision-making process, and there are probably times when this is true. But it is also the case that no data is better than incorrect or misleading data, and if the conclusions reached by the fast-track evaluator are faulty, the court's rulings based on flawed data will also miss the mark. There is an old saying that a quart bottle should give good measure, but should not be expected to hold a gallon. This seems to be the case with fast-track and mini-evaluations, in which clinicians, despite minimal and often inadequate methods, try to address the kinds of questions that traditionally are assessed using the traditional comprehensive methodology. This model is also problematic because it potentially falls short of the APA guidelines and aspirational standards requiring that assessments are adequate to appropriately address the referral question.

## THE ISSUE FOCUSED FORENSIC CHILD CUSTODY ASSESSMENT

Another model of child custody assessment has been variously called the minimalist, problem focused, or issue focused model of assessment. It should be understood that the goal of this model is not to replace the traditional model, but to provide another option for the courts that bridges the gap between the comprehensive and mini-evaluations. As previously mentioned, a number of authors have written about custody evaluations that are focused on a particular problem or issue in a custody case rather than attempting to address global issues such as BIC.

### OVERVIEW OF THE ISSUE FOCUSED FORENSIC MODEL

A number of changes in focus and emphasis characterize this alternative custody evaluation methodology.

1. It is a principle of this methodology that the child custody evaluation should closely follow the applicable state statutes or standards. In cases where a particular standard is nebulous or when there is no closely corresponding psycholegal equivalent, the evaluator should either refrain from giving an opinion about the issue or attempt to operationalize the issue and explicitly state the rationale behind the operationalization.
2. These evaluations are designed to be concise and circumscribed rather than comprehensive. Evaluators utilizing this model do not volunteer opinions that are not specifically related to the questions being asked, but focus instead on issues and questions relevant to the purpose of the evaluation. This approach reduces the risk of overreaching by the evaluator, which may usurp the role of the fact finder. To the extent possible, evaluation

techniques and conclusions are designed to correspond to the specific referral questions posed to the evaluator by the court or guardian ad litem. Although important data needs to be confirmed by other sources where possible, there should be an explicit rationale for the collection of data that underscores its relationship to the issue being assessed.

3. The evaluator's conclusions, stated in reports and testimony, should be based on objective data gathered in the evaluation and should have an explicit logical connection to this data. Although clinical impressions and other data drawn from nonobjective methods have a role in child custody evaluations, such data should generally be used only to generate hypotheses that can be tested more rigorously.

4. Issues in child custody that do not lend themselves to assessment with known reliability and validity should generally not be part of a child custody evaluation. If the guardian ad litem or fact finder can assess a particular issue as well as the evaluator (i.e., cleanliness of the family home), then the assessment of that issue should be left to those parties. To do otherwise can be misleading to the court, because it gives the illusion that the conclusion being rendered is an expert opinion.

5. Conclusions in child custody evaluations should be made at the lowest inferential level possible.

## THE ISSUE FOCUSED FORENSIC CHILD CUSTODY ASSESSMENT: PRACTICAL APPLICATION

The evaluation principles outlined previously provide a framework for performing an issue focused forensic child custody assessment, but the practicing clinician will require more information if he or she is to make use of this model. The New Hampshire courts have made a list of those areas that often require assessment, either by guardians ad litem or mental health professionals. This list has been codified as the Order on Appointment of the Guardian Ad Litem. A form listing the areas that may be assessed is provided to the guardian ad litem, and some or all can be checked off by the presiding justice in the case. These areas for assessment are:

1. Legal custody
2. Primary physical custody/shared custody
3. Visitation/custodial time
4. Special needs of the children
5. Counseling for family/individual counseling for plaintiff/ defendant/children
6. Psychological evaluations of plaintiff/defendant/children
7. Parenting skills of plaintiff/defendant/both parties
8. Appropriateness of the home environment of plaintiff/ defendant/both parties
9. Substance abuse: alcohol/drugs/both/other
10. Violence, physical abuse, emotional abuse
11. Sexual abuse of children
12. Supervision of visitation
13. Rights of grandparents to visit
14. Influence of companions of either party on the children
15. Maturity of children stating a preference
16. Travel arrangements
17. Time, place, and manner of exchange for visits
18. Assessment of bond between each child and each parent and/ or between siblings

This list is fairly straightforward and contains most of the factors that are addressed in other such lists. For example, Schutz et al. (1989) reviewed the laws in all 50 states to determine which custody-related factors reflected a high degree of consensus. Their list of high-consensus factors included the following:

1. Presence of child or spousal abuse
2. Ages and sexes of the children
3. Adjustment of the children to their environment
4. Length of time in their present environment
5. Children's need for special emotional or physical care
6. Economic situation of the parties
7. The children's wishes, if they are of a sufficient age
8. Parents' desires
9. Educational needs of the children
10. Agreement between the parents
11. Separation of the siblings

12. Mental and physical health of the parents
13. Prior custody determinations
14. Hostility levels between parents
15. Flexibility on the part of either parent
16. General parenting skills
17. Religious concerns
18. Caretaking arrangements prior to and after separation
19. Likelihood that custodial parent will move children from the jurisdiction or alienate the affections of the children for the other parent

Consequently, The New Hampshire Order on Appointment of the Guardian Ad Litem form provides a framework from which we can examine how the mental health professional performing a custody evaluation can evaluate (or not evaluate) each factor in a manner that is maximally reliable and helpful to the court or the guardian ad litem.

## LEGAL CUSTODY

Whether evaluators should address the ultimate issue of legal custody is contentious and much debated by legal and mental health professionals. On one hand, many experts feel that evaluators in any legal proceeding, including custody assessments, should avoid giving opinions regarding the ultimate issue. Those supporting this position give a number of compelling arguments. One of these is that the ultimate decision regarding child custody rests with the court, which is empowered by our society to make decisions about custody based on the totality of the information, the weight to be given to each factor, and the judge's own personal values and priorities. Mental health experts are involved in the process for the express purpose of assisting in the court's decision-making process by utilizing techniques and providing information not readily available to laypersons. Nothing in the evaluator's training makes his or her personal opinion about who should have custody any better than the guardian ad litem's or the judge's. In this view, mental health professionals who offer their opinions about the ultimate disposition regarding custody are encroaching on the province of the court.

On the other hand, there is nothing in the rules of evidence that precludes the evaluator from providing an opinion on the issue of legal custody. There is a trend in American divorce courts to allow more and more information from many quarters into evidence. In these proceedings, it is common to hear objections to evidence being admitted answered by the court with "I will admit it, as your objection goes to the weight and not the admissibility." Those who espouse the view that the expert should be allowed to state an opinion regarding legal custody point out that the judge is entitled to ask for the expert's opinion regarding legal custody and can give the opinion great weight, consider it as just another factor, or ignore it entirely.

On a personal note, I have only once been asked directly by a judge while on the stand, "Doctor, should I transfer custody of these children to their father?" I found this experience disturbing for several reasons. First, I have always avoided providing an opinion on legal custody because I generally adhere to the idea that providing such testimony would be overreaching. Secondly, although I am part of the custody process in these cases, there has always been a buffer between me and the ultimate responsibility for the decision of custody, that being the court. In this case, I was able to truthfully tell the judge that I didn't know if the potential negative effects of removing the children from their home, their school, and their mother, who had primarily raised them, would outweigh the positive effects of placing them with their out-of-state father, who was clearly the more stable and effective parent. The judge ultimately left the children with the mother but greatly increased the father's custodial time.

It should be noted that there are several legal custody arrangements. Generally, both parents retain legal custody of their children, meaning that whatever the custody and visitation plan, they both retain important rights. In most cases, noncustodial parents with legal custody still have input into major decisions in areas of their children's lives such as schooling, medical treatment, sports, and so on. Generally, custodial parents have more control over day-to-day decisions by virtue of being primary caretakers. However, there are situations in which full legal and physical custody is granted to one parent. This arrangement can be ordered when the behavior of one parent is so negative that his or her legal rights in relation to the couple's children must be curtailed. This can happen in cases of domestic violence or child abuse, but can also occur when one parent consistently obstructs important processes, such as an education plan for a child with an educational handicap, or stands in the way of appropriate medical treatment.

In these situations, an evaluator utilizing the issue focused forensic model would work primarily as an investigator. He or she could interview the parents and children (if the children are old enough) to obtain information about each parent's view of the situation. Collateral sources such as teachers, day care providers, and medical personnel could be interviewed to document the extent to which one parent or the other parent is being obstructionist. This would provide the court with information about the extent to which the situation presents a significant risk to the children in the case. In some cases, diagnostic psychological assessment may be undertaken to provide the court with information about the extent to which an obstructionist parent's actions are related to psychological problems, as well as opinions as to how likely the situation is to be remediated in a reasonable length of time by psychotherapeutic intervention.

## PRIMARY PHYSICAL CUSTODY/SHARED CUSTODY

As with the issue of legal custody, the determination of which parent should have primary custody, or whether joint physical custody would be the best arrangement for the family, is the province of the court. Consequently, mental health professionals utilizing the issue focused forensic model should avoid giving testimony that addresses the ultimate issue. However, there are aspects of this issue in which the mental health professional may assist the court. For example, many authorities on the subject of joint physical custody have suggested certain factors that are associated with successful joint physical custody, such as the absence of domestic violence, sufficient proximity to make such an arrangement practical, and the ability to put aside personal animosity in order to collaborate in making decisions affecting the welfare of one's children. In addition, a consistent home environment is especially desirable for children who have certain conditions, such as attention-deficit/hyperactivity disorder, Asperger's syndrome, and other emotional or information-processing problems. In these situations, the evaluator can use interviews, collateral contacts, and record review to assess the parents' level of cooperation prior to and during the divorce. In addition, when the child's adaptation to joint custody is an issue due to special needs, this can be addressed through a clinical assessment of the child.

There is one caveat regarding the issue of assessment of suitability for joint custody. Although there is surprisingly little data on the subject, existing research suggests that there is no evidence that children do better in particular custody arrangements or that joint custody is superior to primary custody for one parent and visitation for the other. There are several possible reasons for this. One is that families may self-select arrangements that work for them after the acrimony of the divorce is over, and as a result, those with joint physical custody are satisfied with their outcome, as are those who self-select a more traditional setup. Another, less positive, take on these findings is that most of the negative effects of divorce come from the impact of the divorce itself (the dissolution of the parental unit), and that what one does afterwards by way of custody/visitation accounts for only a small percentage of the outcome variance. A third, and to my mind fascinating, possibility is raised by DeClue (2002), in his article entitled "The Best Interests of the Village Children." In this article, DeClue notes that there is an implicit belief in the child custody literature that if everyone parented properly, eschewed substance abuse and domestic violence, and kept their children away from violent video games, the vast majority of children would grow up to be upstanding, law-abiding, well-adjusted, tax-paying citizens. DeClue reviews recent research suggesting that personality is formed primarily by genetics (temperament) and a child's social environment, with the parent-child interaction making a small contribution to the total outcome variance. This would suggest that differences in parenting style or custody arrangements are less important to outcome than is generally thought to be the case.

## VISITATION/CUSTODIAL TIME

As with Item 1, legal custody, and Item 2, primary physical custody/shared custody, visitation/custodial time is primarily a legal issue which does not lend itself to psychological assessment in most cases. Whether children should see their noncustodial parent from Friday afternoon through Sunday night or from Saturday morning through Sunday afternoon, or whether a dinner on Wednesday should be allowed on a weekly basis will be decided primarily on the basis of the guardian ad litem's or judge's values and lifestyle preferences. Psychological science per se (at least as matters presently stand) has relatively little to contribute due to the paucity of empirical research in this area. The mental health professional may assist the court by reviewing research related to the issue at hand, such as overnight visitation for preschool-aged children or the relative merits of short, frequent visits versus longer, less frequent visits.

## SPECIAL NEEDS OF THE CHILDREN

This is an area in which the mental health professional can be very helpful to the guardian and court. As previously mentioned, any number of conditions and related special needs may be affected by divorce and may need to be considered when determining custody and visitation arrangements. In some cases, these conditions and needs may have already been diagnosed. This can be the case when the child already has a psychotherapist or has been coded as educationally handicapped by his or her school district. In other cases, a child's special needs and problems may not come to the fore until the family comes under outside scrutiny in the divorce, or when the child begins to demonstrate behavioral/emotional problems during the divorce. Whatever the case, a number of steps should be considered in the assessment of children's special needs.

- The parents should be interviewed and a careful developmental history taken. Any number of developmental history forms are available for this purpose. For example, I have parents complete the Developmental History Checklist for Children (Dougherty & Schinka, 1989), either in advance of their appointment or when they arrive at the office. The Developmental History form has an associated software program which allows the evaluator or office staff to enter the parents' responses into the program and output a narrative report. This report can be edited and pasted into the final report. This is helpful if the evaluator does a high volume of assessments, but the form can also be used without the software. It can be utilized as an interview driver, and any unusual responses can be questioned further.
- The evaluator should obtain and review any collateral information that might bear on the referral issue. This could include the results of previous evaluations by clinicians or school evaluators, notes from the child's therapist (or direct discussion with the therapist), or any other records that might cast light on diagnostic issues.

- Parent clinical interviews are also important to learn the particulars of a child's level of adjustment as well as the nature of any manifest problems. This allows the evaluator to explore the situations that concern the parents or, alternately, ask questions about situations that have been raised by the court. It also provides the evaluator with information about if and how the child's behavior and emotional responses are seen differently by each parent.

- At least one interview with the child is recommended, although in contested custody situations it is best to have the child brought in by each parent for a separate interview. I find it best to utilize both structured and unstructured approaches to interviewing. Many structured child clinical interviews are available, but I find the Children's Interview for Psychiatric Syndromes (ChIPS; E. B. Weller et al., 1999) very useful and easy to use. It covers a large age range (preschool to 18 years), is closely tied to *DSM-IV-TR* (American Psychiatric Association, 2000) diagnostic criteria, and has a branching structure that allows the interviewer to move to the next diagnostic category quickly if the entry criteria for the diagnostic area being assessed are not met. Depending on the child's age, drawing or a game can be used as a focusing activity and questions can be asked while the child is so engaged.

- Psychological testing may be utilized to aid in diagnosis and as a check on the evaluator's clinical impressions. The type of testing will vary with the referral question.

If the referral question relates to the child's intellectual abilities or to learning process deficits, the evaluator should consider whether he or she has the expertise to perform such testing, or whether that part of the assessment should be referred to a colleague with background in psychoeducational assessment. Because my doctorate is in school psychology, I am comfortable doing my own assessment in this area. The Wechsler Intelligence Scale for Children-Fourth Edition (WISC-IV; Wechsler, 2003) and Wechsler Adult Intelligence Scale-Third Edition (WAIS-III; Wechsler, 1998) are probably considered the gold standard for intellectual assessment, but I have recently begun using the Reynolds Intellectual Assessment Scales (RIAS; Reynolds & Kamphaus, 2003). The RIAS has a number of advantages over the

Wechsler scales. In the RIAS, Cecil Reynolds has moved away from the ipsative comparisons of subtests that are so much a part of the traditional interpretation of the WISC and WAIS, believing (along with many other authorities on the subject) that the Wechsler subtests are simply not robust enough to support such usage. The RIAS is shorter than the Wechsler scales and provides the equivalent of Verbal, Performance, and Full scale IQs. It also supplies a Memory scale that is not utilized in computing the Full scale IQ but may provide useful information about problems in that area.

IQ screening tests are also available and may be appropriate, depending on the situation. The Kaufman Brief Intelligence Test, Second Edition (KBIT-2; A. S. Kaufman & N. L. Kaufman, 2004), is short but reasonably well normed and constructed, and the Wechsler Abbreviated Scale of Intelligence (WASI; Wechsler, 1999) is a short form of the WISC and WAIS. The RIAS also has a short form made up of two subtests from the longer form.

There are a number of academic achievement batteries on the market, providing different degrees of detail regarding a particular child's educational progress. The Woodcock-Johnson III (McGrew & Woodcock, 2001) is comprehensive and widely used, and it includes a cognitive ability section that may be used in lieu of the IQ tests mentioned above. Disadvantages include the fact that it cannot be hand scored; computer scoring software from the manufacturer must be used. It is also quite lengthy and complicated to administer. The Wechsler Individual Achievement Test-Second Edition (WIAT-II; Wechsler, 2002) from Harcourt Assessment (formally the Psychological Corporation) is also quite comprehensive and has the advantage of having been developed specifically to be used with the Wechsler IQ tests, although it can be used independently or with other IQ tests as well. In addition to providing standard and percentile scores for domains such as Reading Comprehension, Math Computation, and Writing, the WIAT also includes a number of optional process measurements which the evaluator can use if desired, depending on his or her needs and approach to testing. Shorter achievement tests are also available in cases where a screening measure is appropriate. The Wide Range Achievement Test 4 (WRAT-4; Wilkinson & Robertson, 2005) including Reading Recognition, Math Computation, and Spelling for adults and children are good choices when a less comprehensive assessment is required.

Finally, personality tests and behavior rating scales may be appropriate to provide further information about a child or adolescent's emotional functioning and adjustment. For younger children and adolescents, the Behavior Assessment System for Children, Second Edition (BASC-2; Reynolds & Kamphaus, 2004), provides three forms: Child Self Report, Parent Report, and Teacher Report. All three forms are available for age groups from preschool to adolescent, with the exception of the self-report form for the youngest group, who would not be able to read the questions. The BASC-2 provides scales that measure psychopathology such as Depression, Anxiety, Conduct Problems, and Hyperactivity, and also provides adaptive scales that measure Adaptability, Leadership, and Adult and Peer Relations. The BASC-2 is also one of the few tests of its type that has validity scales that measure inconsistency as well as positive and negative impression trends. It can be given in paper-and-pencil format, but can also be administered by computer and scored immediately. It can be illuminating to use the alternate forms to compare each parent's views about the child's emotional problems to those of the other parent and the child's teachers.

The Conners' Rating Scales-Revised (CRS-R; Conners, 1997) covers similar domains as the BASC-2, comes in a variety of long and short parent, teacher, and adolescent self-report forms, and can be computer scored. The Personality Inventory for Children, Second Edition (PIC-2; Wirt et al., 2001) is another useful child and adolescent assessment tool.

A number of self-report inventories can be utilized with adolescents. The Minnesota Multiphasic Personality Inventory-Adolescent (MMPI-A; Butcher, Williams, et al., 2001) is very comprehensive and well constructed and can be administered by computer, but many adolescents balk at the length. The Millon Adolescent Clinical Inventory (MACI; T. Millon, 1993) is much shorter and, in my experience, is better tolerated for this reason. The Jesness Inventory-Revised (JI-R; Jesness, 1996) can be used with children as young as 9. Although it is commonly used with children who are delinquent, it can be used with nondelinquent children as well.

I do not recommend the use of projective tests in forensic assessments generally and in custody assessments specifically. An in-depth discussion of the utility of instruments such as Exner's Comprehensive System for the Rorschach (CS; Exner, 2003) and other projective measures is beyond the scope of this book, and those who are interested should review the voluminous and at times acrimonious literature on the subject. In brief, from my perspective, projective tests have several disadvantages in custody assessments:

- They add little information or incremental validity to the information provided by a careful history, mental status examination, record review, and objective testing.
- They have little (if any) direct bearing on the specific types of questions raised in custody assessments.
- Their test format is an inefficient way of gathering data.
- They lend themselves to overinterpretation.
- The controversy surrounding them makes them easy to attack in court.

Once the necessary steps have been taken to assess a child's special needs, the evaluator can integrate the data to provide the court with the following information:

- Whether the child has special needs which might be affected by postdivorce disposition.
- The nature of those needs.
- The evaluator's opinions about the type of services, therapy, home environment, and other considerations that will be important for the court to consider in determining custody and visitation.

## COUNSELING FOR FAMILY/INDIVIDUAL COUNSELING FOR PLAINTIFF/DEFENDANT/CHILDREN

Clearly, this item is partially subsumed under Item 4, special needs of the children, and Item 6, psychological evaluations of plaintiff/defendant/children, but the focus is slightly different. Put simply, Item 6 is the court's way of asking "What is the matter with these folks?" and often arises out of the court's concern that one or more of the parties' behavior suggests the possibility of psychological problems. Implicit in Item 5 is "What do we do about these problems?" In my experience, this issue is raised when the court wants information about the remediablity of observed adjustment or behavior problems in parents or their children through individual, group, or family therapy.

Obviously, good therapy follows from good diagnosis, and judgments about whether specific treatments are indicated and the likelihood that they will improve the adaptation of one or all of the parties requires good case formulation. The evaluator may determine that a child in a divorce has an adjustment disorder related to family upheaval. In such a case, referral to a child therapist experienced in working with children of divorce for supportive counseling may be appropriate. If the child exhibits more serious psychopathology, either preexisting or exacerbated by divorce, referral to a specialist may be warranted. In my experience, family therapy is unlikely to be effective during the custody dispute, because there is a strong likelihood that material revealed in therapy will be used by one or the other parents to obtain an advantage in the proceedings. Additionally, tensions during the actual custody battle are often too high to allow the formation of a workable therapeutic alliance. Such therapy may be useful after the divorce is finalized and there is some return to baseline functioning.

In other cases, the parents will be the focus of this question. It will be important to determine what type of problem exists and the amenability of that problem to psychotherapeutic intervention. For example, the evaluator may determine that a mother's severe depressive episode is reactive in nature, responded well to antidepressants, and has been under control for an extended period of time. In such a case, the evaluator may recommend to the court that the mother's continued monthly meetings with her psychiatrist are sufficient to assure the court that a recurrence of symptoms is unlikely and that the court need not be overly concerned about this facet of the case. In other cases, it may be determined that a father's problematic behavior and refusal to cooperate with his ex-wife in the interest of their children may be related to a severe narcissistic personality disorder. In such a case, the evaluator may conclude that the father's condition is likely to be difficult to treat even if he is seen by a therapist who specializes in the treatment of personality disorders. This may help the court decide that an approach that limits the negative impact of the father's personality and behaviors is best when determining the amount and form of custodial time, and also not to expect that the behaviors of concern will stop in the foreseeable future, even with psychotherapy.

In some cases, issues related to substance abuse, domestic violence, and sexual abuse may be indicated. These issues will be covered later in this section.

## PSYCHOLOGICAL EVALUATIONS OF PLAINTIFF/DEFENDANT/CHILDREN

As mentioned in the discussion of Item 5, counseling for family/ individual counseling for plaintiff/defendant/children, appropriate diagnosis of the parties can assist the court in determining various aspects of postdivorce arrangements. Evaluation of the children has already been addressed in the discussion of Item 4, special needs of the children. Adult diagnostic evaluations in the issue focused forensic model can be requested for a number of reasons. The issue of one parent's past mental health history may be brought up in the course of the divorce proceedings, and the court or guardian may wish to have information about that individual's current psychological status. This type of assessment may also be requested due to charges and countercharges made by the divorcing couple against each other. In a recent case, the court ordered an evaluation of the father in a custody dispute. The father had been inappropriately angry with the guardian and somewhat arrogant in his approach to the court, and his self-defeating behavior raised concerns that this might somehow affect his ability to care for his infant son. The guardian was sensitive to the fact that the stress of the divorce might be driving the father's behavior, as opposed to some type of ingrained behavior pattern, but the court wanted the reassurance of a psychological assessment.

My preference, and the preference of many other custody evaluators, is to avoid evaluating only one party in custody matters. The main problem with evaluating only one member of the divorcing couple is that any less-than-perfect aspects of that parent's personality can be seized upon by opposing counsel, while the party who was not evaluated does not have to undergo the same type of scrutiny. I have called this the "sauce for the goose" principle; if Mom has to take the MMPI-2, then Dad should take it, too. However, in some cases the parties agree that one parent should be evaluated and not the other for a specific reason, or such an evaluation is requested by the court in particular circumstances. In such cases it is important that the evaluator lay out the parameters and limitations of the evaluation with particular care. He or she should specifically state the purpose of the evaluation. For example, the evaluator might include the following statement in the report:

Three years ago Ms. Smith was briefly hospitalized for what was diagnosed as postpartum depression subsequent to the birth of her son. The court has requested an evaluation of Ms. Smith's current level of psychological adjustment to determine whether she suffers from psychopathology of a type and severity which could compromise her parenting ability. The court is also interested in whether Ms. Smith's previous symptoms are likely to recur. This assessment is not intended to compare the parenting abilities of Ms. Smith with those of her husband. Conclusions will be based on a mental status examination, a clinical interview, objective personality testing, a review of her past psychiatric records, and telephonic contact with Ms. Smith's current psychotherapist and her employer.

Such a statement protects both the client and the evaluator. Inadequate specificity at the outset of such assessment can lead to the misuse of the report produced by the evaluator, and can also lead to complaints to the local licensing board.

In my experience, there are four indispensable components of a psychological evaluation performed in the context of a custody proceeding. These include a review of collateral information, a mental status evaluation, a clinical interview, and psychological testing.

The first component, a review of collateral information, may include a review of mental health and employment records, discussions with past and present therapists, and other contacts as appropriate. Although it is important to be thorough and to gather any information that is likely to have an impact on the evaluator's conclusions, the information requested should have a direct bearing on the referral question. My approach to assessments in the context of a custody evaluation is to provide a picture of current functioning and not necessarily to provide an exhaustive history of all psychological problems an individual may have had in the past. Consequently, if a 25-year-old man had 6 months of psychotherapy at the age of 16 and then had no further contact with mental health professionals until he developed an addiction to Vicodan subsequent to a back injury at age 23, it is not always necessary to attempt to obtain the adolescent psychotherapy records. Professional judgment must be utilized in this regard.

A mental status evaluation (MSE) is another essential component of psychological evaluations when custody is an issue. Although it is rarely appropriate to omit this procedure in performing forensic evaluations, evaluators should use their judgment in determining what type of MSE to administer. If the referral issue includes indications that organicity or a thought disorder may be present, a "hard-core," formal MSE should be utilized. In cases where these issues are unlikely to be present, a more general mental status examination can be utilized. For formal mental status examinations, Psychological Assessment Resources, Inc. (PAR; www.parinc.com) publishes mental status checklists for adults, children, and adolescents which can be very useful as interview drivers. I use these checklists with almost every patient who sees me for an evaluation, asking the questions directly from the form in the first part of my interview. The structure of the checklists helps patients to relax, because answering questions in this format is generally less stressful than trying to decide what the evaluator needs to hear. The checklist can be used as a consumable booklet and the answers dictated later, or the client's answers can be entered into PAR's software, which outputs a narrative report that can be edited to fit the evaluator's writing style. Although this format suits my needs, selecting a mental status examination is up to the evaluator's preferences, and other options are available from various publishers.

The third component of forensic psychological evaluations, a clinical interview, allows the evaluator to question the client informally about issues related to the referral question. In most cases, this involves taking a personal history (including information about the client's family of origin, educational history, social and occupational roles, and relationships) as well as exploring any history of mental-health-related issues if appropriate. This book is not intended to provide in-depth coverage of clinical interviewing techniques, and it is assumed that those undertaking issue focused forensic child custody work will be well-versed in this aspect of personality assessment. However, the use of structured or semistructured inventories can be quite helpful in ensuring that all pertinent information is gathered. Some practitioners may prefer to utilize one of the commercially available structured clinical interview forms, such as Wiley's, or one of the various forms provided in Sattler's (1998) book, *Clinical and Forensic Interviewing of Children and Families*. Other practitioners may prefer to have the client fill out a personal history form, such as PAR's Personal History Checklist for Adults (PHC; Shinka, 1989), prior to the interview and review it during a face-to-face session with the client. Having the client fill out such a history form has certain advantages. Given the sometimes contentious nature of forensic work in this area of practice, it may be prudent to have evidence that a client has or has not been forthright about issues such as arrests, drug use, and treatment, and also that the clinician took steps to question the client directly about these and other issues.

The fourth essential component of psychological evaluations when custody is an issue is psychological testing. As previously mentioned, in forensic contexts my preference is to employ the best objective testing available. I believe it is best to avoid projective tests in forensic work for a number of reasons. All projective techniques except the Exner CS Rorschach have serious and well-documented problems related to their lack of reliability and validity. The Exner CS Rorschach has become increasingly controversial, but regardless of whether the pro-Rorschach or the anti-Rorschach camp is correct about the test, defending the use of the test on cross-examination takes up time and energy which I believe can be more profitably spent in other pursuits.

Virtually every patient I see for forensic assessment of any kind receives the Minnesota Multiphase Personality Inventory-2 (MMPI-2; Butcher, Graham, et al., 2001) and this includes issue focused forensic child custody assessments. The MMPI-2 has the advantage of decades of research and is the most widely accepted psychological test among custody evaluators. In addition, it allows for the development of diagnostic hypotheses which can be checked against the information derived from the mental status examination, clinical interview, and collateral data. It can be administered with paper and pencil, but in my experience the best way to administer and score the test is to utilize the Microtest-Q software available from Pearson Assessments (www.pearsonassessments.com). Such administration is faster, easier, and more accurate than hand scoring. Pearson provides both profile and narrative reports. Many experienced forensic psychologists have cautioned against the use of "canned" narrative reports, and I generally agree with them. Several problems can arise when utilizing narrative reports. One of these is that the psychologist utilizing the narrative report tends to become locked into the report's descriptions and conclusions. Although the psychologist may decide to disregard elements of a computerized report, such as a mention of psychotic tendencies, based on other sources of data, the computerized narrative report is likely to be seen by attorneys involved in the case. The evaluator may be confronted with these statements in court, and their omission from the final report may be taken as evidence of bias on the evaluator's part. Another problematic practice is cutting and pasting whole sections of the computer-generated narrative report into the psychologist's report, which raises issues related to plagiarism and copyright violations. This practice is acceptable, however, with computer-generated mental status and personal history reports, which are designed to be used in this manner. Finally, most psychologists who utilize such reports have no idea how the interpretive statements are derived or whether they are the product of empirical research, clinical judgment, or the experience of whoever designed the software. Sophisticated attorneys will be sure to bring this lack of knowledge to the attention of the trier of fact.

However, some psychologists hold that the use of computer-generated narrative reports, even in forensic cases, is defensible. Their contention is that all of the data gathered help generate hypotheses related to the ultimate diagnosis, and the data are ultimately weighed and utilized according to the psychologist's clinical judgment and experience. In addition, they point out that evaluators who do not utilize computer-generated narrative reports generally utilize similar "canned" statements from authoritative texts on the MMPI-2, and that the only difference is the lack of a printed record in the file. Ultimately, it is a matter of professional experience and judgment whether or not to use these computer-generated reports. However, in my experience they create more problems than they solve in forensic cases.

It should be noted that research indicates that custody litigants who are administered the MMPI-2 show a marked trend toward defensiveness. This tendency is so common that some authors have called for the development of custody-specific norms for interpretation of the MMPI-2. Other researchers have suggested that custody litigants are no more or less defensive than other forensic clients. In any case, clinicians should not be surprised to find high levels of defensive responding on the MMPI-2 and other objective tests administered in this context.

The Personality Assessment Inventory (PAI; Morey, 1991) is gaining popularity as a forensic instrument. Some clinicians have switched from the MMPI-2 to the PAI, and I believe it is a useful test in custody-related evaluations. It can also be utilized when the MMPI-2 has been recently administered and there is a need for further diagnostic testing. This can occur when the diagnostic evaluation is being done to provide a second opinion. The PAI can also be administered online, and for clinicians who do a high volume of testing it may be more economical than the MMPI-2 due to the lower cost of individual administrations.

The Millon Clinical Multiaxial Inventory-III (MCMI-III; T. Millon, David, & C. Millon, 1997) is frequently used in diagnostic evaluations because it is thought to be more sensitive to personality disorders than the MMPI-2 and the PAI. The use of the MCMI-III with custody litigants has been controversial, because the test was mainly normed on a clinical population. In addition, some research indicates that custody litigants produce profiles with elevated defensiveness on the validity scales of the MCMI-III as well as elevations on the Compulsive, Histrionic, and Narcissistic scales. There is some question as to whether these elevations are an accurate reflection of custody litigants' characteristics or an artifact of their defensive approach to the instrument. Some have argued that this triad of elevations is characteristic of individuals who cannot resolve custody and parenting issues in a productive manner, and that they are therefore overrepresented in the population of those referred for mental health evaluations in custody matters. Mental health professionals who choose to utilize the MCMI-III should be familiar with the literature in this area and be prepared to defend the use of the test in court.

Once the information outlined above has been gathered, the clinician can compose the report. The scope of the conclusions depends on the referral question; in some cases only a report detailing one or both parents' level of psychopathology or lack thereof is requested, and in other cases it is understood from the outset that the relationship between any observed adjustment difficulties and their potential impact on parenting ability will be explored. In the latter case, I recommend that the bar be set high and that relatively mild problems not be overinterpreted with regard to their potential impact on the family's children. I make this suggestion for a number of pragmatic reasons. First, there is little solid research indicating that many forms of parental psychopathology are robustly related to poor outcomes in children. Clearly, debilitating forms of psychopathology can cause what I have referred to as gross parenting incapacity. In many cases, schizophrenia, bipolar disorder, or severe recurrent depression can be refractory to treatment and can undercut the afflicted parent's ability to provide minimally acceptable parenting. In the same way, severe personality disorders (antisocial, borderline, narcissistic) can create so many problems that the afflicted parent cannot be given the main responsibility for parenting. However, I believe that it is important for the evaluator to remember that millions of children have parents who have experienced depression, posttraumatic stress disorder (PTSD), obsessive-compulsive disorder (OCD), or anxiety disorders, yet are parenting effectively every day. If every parent who had ever been in therapy or placed on a selective serotonin reuptake inhibitor were deemed unfit, there would not be enough "normal" adults to parent their children. Consequently, evaluators should interpret their results conservatively and be circumspect about basing any statements to the court regarding parenting capacity on the results of a circumscribed psychological evaluation. Consistent with the APA ethical code, evaluators' conclusions should be based closely on the data.

## PARENTING SKILLS OF PLAINTIFF/DEFENDANT/BOTH PARTIES

In general, an evaluation of parenting skills is best addressed utilizing comprehensive custody assessment methodology. This is because the issue is broad and a great deal of information is required to address it appropriately. In order to assess the comparative parenting abilities of both adult parties, a number of important areas have to be explored. A complete review of each parent's history and practices in rearing children must be obtained, and in many instances attempts have to be made to corroborate each parent's self-report. Observations of parent-child interaction are required, as well as review of collateral data (school and medical reports) and interviews with third parties such as day care teachers, guidance counselors, relatives, and neighbors. Interviews with the children are also generally necessary, and testing of the parents and children might also be utilized.

In some cases the court or guardian may approach the evaluator with specific questions about a parent's general knowledge of parenting, including the developmental needs of children, attitudes toward discipline and/or corporal punishment, or other issues that may be helpful in a specific case. For example, in my practice I have received this type of request in assessments of young or inexperienced parents. In one case, a very young, unmarried couple had an infant who was the product of an unplanned pregnancy. The infant resided with her mother and the maternal grandmother, who were quite protective of her and were reluctant to allow the father to interact with her outside of their household. The guardian ad litem had thoroughly explored the background and personal history of the father and had determined that there was no evidence of criminality, mental illness, substance abuse, or other obvious factors that would preclude the possibility of unsupervised, or even overnight, visitation between father and daughter.

The guardian requested that I assess the father to provide information about his emotional stability and knowledge of the needs of very young children. I interviewed the father, performed a mental status examination, and administered the MMPI-2 and the MCMI-III to address the emotional stability component of the referral. In addition, I administered the Adult-Adolescent Parenting Inventory-2 (AAPI-2; Bavolek & Keene, 1999) and the Child Abuse Potential Inventory (CAPI; Milner, 1986). The AAPI-2 is an objective test that provides information about a parent's stated attitudes regarding corporal punishment, role reversal, empathy, and related issues. It should be noted that the AAPI-2 has no validity scales, and many of the items are face valid, so although it can determine whether a parent is aware of appropriate parenting practices, it cannot detect whether he or she actually employs these practices. For example, a parent who relies exclusively on spanking to discipline his or her children could mislead the examiner by stating on the form that he or she strongly values alternatives to corporal punishment. For this reason, I recommend that the AAPI-2 be used only to determine whether a parent can articulate appropriate parenting attitudes. In my experience, if a parent obtains low scores on the AAPI-2 it is likely that he or she has significant deficiencies in parenting ability—parents who cannot at least "talk the talk" will almost certainly not be able to "walk the walk." Put another way, the AAPI-2 can assist in ruling in skill and knowledge deficiencies in a parent, but cannot rule them out.

The CAPI is a surprisingly robust instrument for detecting attitudes correlated with physical abuse of children in a population in which the base rate of such behavior is high. In this particular case, the father had no parenting history on which to base any type of predictions of future behavior. However, based on my assessment I was able to provide the guardian with information indicating that the father had no psychopathology which, in and of itself, would raise questions about his parenting ability. Additionally, I was able to state in my report that the father articulated appropriate parenting attitudes and did not appear to have any predisposition to be physically abusive to small children in his care. I was clear about the limitations of the instruments and also stated that the results of my testing needed to be considered in the context of the information gathered by the guardian. In this case the court provided the father initially with short periods of unsupervised visitation which were gradually expanded to include overnights.

The parenting skills portion of the issue focused forensic assessment is often, but not always, combined with the psychological evaluations of the parents, but it covers different areas of functioning. The focus of parenting assessment relates closely to what Grisso (2003) has termed the functional assessment. In Grisso's protocol for the assessment of competencies, the first step is a determination of the client's ability to perform the behaviors that are the focus of the assessment. In a competency to stand trial assessment, the focus of the functional component of the assessment is whether the defendant has a sufficient factual and rational understanding of the trial process and sufficient ability to consult with his or her attorney with a reasonable degree of factual and rational understanding.

If deficits are noted, the next component of Grisso's model is the *causal* component. Put simply, this means that the evaluator attempts to discover the cause of the observed problem. For example, a defendant may demonstrate significant deficits in her grasp of the major issues involved in standing trial. The evaluator may need to investigate conditions such as mental retardation, neurological impairment, psychosis, or malingering to help explain observed deficits.

The interactive (person/situation congruence) component of the assessment considers the subject's strengths and weaknesses in the context of the situation at hand. For example, the defendant in a competency case might be considered competent in a simple case of assault in which his testimony is unlikely to be required, but might be unable to perform as well in a more complicated drug possession case in which there are multiple defendants, complicated issues of law, and a need to testify and therefore be cross-examined.

Grisso terms the next step the conclusory component, and it is in this section of the evaluation that the expert presents his or her opinions regarding the findings. There is a good deal of controversy in forensic psychology regarding whether it is proper for the evaluator to give an opinion regarding the ultimate issue, or the issue before the court. Statements declaring that a defendant is believed to be competent, reliable, not guilty by reason of insanity, or a better parent than the other party are examples of ultimate issue opinions. Many experts feel that experts should avoid giving such testimony because these matters are legal rather than psychological in nature, while others believe the judge or jury can give such testimony whatever weight they consider appropriate.

Lastly, the evaluator may provide opinions related to the remediative component, which addresses whether intervention could make a difference in the defendant's or litigant's competency. For example, many individuals who are incompetent due to acute psychosis can be restored to competence with medication, while those who have deficits due to mental retardation are unlikely to have their underlying condition remediated.

In the case of parenting evaluations, a number of techniques and instruments can be utilized. A thorough history provides the context for the assessment. Parents should be interviewed about their parenting experience with the child in question as well as their experience with other children. Many custody evaluators utilize checklists and questionnaires to streamline this process and ensure that all areas are covered thoroughly. These questionnaires can be mailed to the parent before the face-to-face interview, because they are not tests, and using them in this way will not compromise their integrity. A number of such forms are available commercially, including the Parenting History Survey (PHS) and the Uniform Child Custody Evaluation System (UCCES; Munsinger & Karlson, 1994). The Parenting History Survey is very comprehensive and also quite inexpensive; it can be purchased for a small one-time fee which entitles the purchaser to unlimited use. (It can be obtained by contacting Stuart Greenberg, PhD, ABPP [Forensic], 1217 24th Avenue E., Seattle, WA 98112.) The Uniform Child Custody Evaluation System, available from PAR, is an extensive collection of forms designed to structure a comprehensive custody assessment. The evaluator can use any of the forms he or she considers relevant to the evaluation.

## APPROPRIATENESS OF THE HOME ENVIRONMENT OF PLAINTIFF/DEFENDANT/BOTH PARTIES

In my experience the issues associated with the appropriateness of the home environment are generally addressed by the guardian. This is a good example of an issue in which the opinions of mental health professionals are often no better than those of laypersons with experience in child rearing. Nothing in the training of psychologists makes them better qualified than others as judges of housekeeping, baby-proofing, or safety of the physical environment. Frankly, my mother would likely be a better judge of these issues than I would, because she raised five children to adulthood and was a homemaker exclusively for the first three. This is not to say that mental health professionals could not perform this role as part of an assessment, but it would be an expensive way to address an issue that a court appointed guardian could easily undertake. It should be noted that some mental health professionals who perform comprehensive custody assessments do make home visits. This allows them to observe parent-child interactions in the home environment. This is one valid way of approaching that type of assessment, and there is no reason why the mental health professionals should not observe and comment on the appropriateness of the physical environment under those circumstances.

## SUBSTANCE ABUSE: ALCOHOL/DRUGS/BOTH/OTHER

Assessment of substance abuse is a specialized area, and mental health professionals who undertake such evaluations should have specialized training and experience in that area. I am frequently asked to perform this type of evaluation, and it lends itself to the issue focused forensic model. Allegations of substance abuse are common in custody disputes, and although they sometimes reflect a very real drug or alcohol problem, in other cases normal patterns of alcohol consumption, or occasional marijuana use, can be exaggerated and used against one of the parties. In either case, assessment of substance abuse in custody situations is, for the most part, the same as such assessments in other contexts. Unfortunately, no psychological test can reliably rule in or rule out substance abuse. In these types of evaluations it is important to obtain any records that might bear on the issue. For example, the evaluator should have a criminal background check done to see if the individual being evaluated has a history of driving while intoxicated (DWI) or reckless operation (terms may vary from jurisdiction to jurisdiction), as well as disorderly conduct or related charges. Although such charges are not proof of a substance abuse problem, DWI convictions are robustly correlated with alcohol abuse, and more than one is virtually all the information needed to make the diagnosis.

Interviewing the client about his or her drug and alcohol use helps the evaluator to put the individual's use of drugs or alcohol in chronological context. For example, it is relatively common for young men to use drugs or alcohol fairly heavily in college or in the military, but moderating their use when in their 30s. To the extent possible, the client's self-report should be corroborated by any collateral sources of data utilized. Work records can be scrutinized and employers contacted, and individuals who know the client but are not partisans can be interviewed. A multitude of tests and inventories are used to assess drug and alcohol use, including the Michigan Alcohol Screening Test (MAST; Selzer, 1971), the Mortimer-Filkins (Mortimer et al., 1971), and a variety of other instruments. Unfortunately, the self-report inventories are face valid, so that anyone who wishes to deny excessive use of alcohol or drugs can do so with ease. As with the AAPI-2, they can be used to rule substance abuse problems in, but are not very effective at ruling them out. Another deficiency in many of these instruments is that they do not place substance abuse in a chronological context. For example, the MAST asks questions in the format "Have you ever. . . ?" The problem is that someone might have been a heavy drinker up to the age of 25 and then abstained completely for the next decade, but he or she would still have a high score on the MAST.

A number of non-face-valid instruments have some utility in these types of evaluations. The MAC-2 scale of the MMPI-2 has some ability to detect personality traits associated with substance abuse, but it cannot be used to diagnose such a problem in isolation. The Substance Abuse Subtle Screening Inventory-3 (SASSI-3; F. Miller et al., 1997) is an objective test that is purported to have some ability to detect substance use disorders in defensive individuals, but there has been research to suggest that the test does not perform as well in this regard as was originally suggested. On the positive side, the SASSI-3 is at least as accurate as tests such as the MAST, and it has the advantage of allowing the evaluator to specify a time frame for the face valid part of the inventory. This can be helpful in assessing individuals who have received substance abuse treatment or quit on their own. Another test, the Research Institute on Addictions Self Inventory (RIASI; Nochajski & B. A. Miller, 1995), has shown a reasonable ability to detect substance abuse problems in defensive individuals. The developers utilize questions in the inventory that are highly correlated with substance abuse problems but are non-face-valid. The test is used by the State of New York in its impaired driver intervention programs and can be helpful in performing substance use evaluations in custody assessments.

It should be noted that assessing substance abuse in the context of a custody evaluation might present issues that typically do not arise in noncustody cases. In a given case, the chief issue may not be a parent's overall consumption of alcohol, but rather whether he or she drinks excessively while the child is in his or her custody or during visitation. For example, a young father may drink five or six beers on noncustodial weekends while playing softball with friends. Under some guidelines, five or six drinks constitute a binge. However, if the father abstains from alcohol during visits, his drinking may not be an issue with reference to child custody matters.

## VIOLENCE, PHYSICAL ABUSE, EMOTIONAL ABUSE, AND SEXUAL ABUSE OF CHILDREN

These areas of assessment present the evaluator with similar issues and many of the same problems. They differ from the other areas of assessment in that they are crimes and not merely areas of concern to the court. This fact has several implications for mental health professionals. The first is that crimes are best investigated by individuals empowered by the state to conduct such investigations. In addition, reports of violence and abuse are almost always reported in the first instance to the police or to local child protective service agencies, and as a consequence a custody evaluator will generally not be called upon as a "first responder." Also, psychologists and other mental health professionals have no tests, techniques, or innate abilities that allow them to determine whether a particular act of abuse or violence has or has not occurred. As has often been pointed out, even the most experienced mental health professionals are not human lie detectors. Because such a role is outside the mental health professional's area of expertise, it would be inappropriate to take it on.

That being said, under certain circumstances allegations of domestic violence or child abuse may become one of the issues in a custody evaluation. This can occur for a number of reasons. For example, some child protection agencies, which are often overburdened, have an unfortunate tendency to dump cases into divorce courts if the allegations arise during divorce proceedings. In addition, after allegations arise, divorce courts often order supervised visitation or curtail visitation entirely between the child and the accused parent. Because the parent is now out of the household and a judge is managing the case, child protection agencies sometimes take the position that child protection has been ensured and the court can sort out the situation on the basis of the evidence presented. In my experience, this is particularly likely to happen when allegations concern less severe forms of abuse. This issue can also arise when domestic violence or child abuse is alleged to have occurred in the past but was not reported at the time. In such cases, the absence of any corroboration of abuse and the lack of a con-temporaneous report can lead to allegations being unfounded. However, it must be understood that in many divorce courts the rules of evidence governing criminal cases do not apply. Many domestic relations judges allow testimony about allegations of past abuse or violence to be brought into court, and judges may respond to objections by saying that the objections go to the weight of the evidence and not to its admissibility. In other words, the testimony is allowed, but the judge will take any objections into consideration in deciding how much importance to give the evidence. For this reason, a custody evaluator may sometimes be put in the position of being asked to investigate such allegations as part of an evaluation.

It goes without saying that any mental health professional who performs such investigations needs to be knowledgeable and experienced in this area. It has been my experience that this is one of the areas in which mental health professionals often rely on junk science, including invalid profiles and checklists of signs and symptoms that are "consistent with" child abuse or domestic violence. Though such techniques lack a scintilla of scientific validity, some psychologists and other professionals are more than willing to come into court and testify on their basis that a particular father or mother has the psychological characteristics of a batterer, or that a child's observed symptoms are consistent with child abuse. Such testimony is, in my opinion, wildly irresponsible and unprofessional and should not be permitted. At the same time, evaluators with the requisite background and experience in child abuse and domestic violence can provide information that is useful to the court in these matters.

Evaluations in this type of case can involve interviews of the parties (both accusing and accused parent and children) as well as any reliable individuals with independent knowledge of the family and children, such as neighbors, teachers, pediatricians, and therapists. The information gleaned from careful interviews can be presented to the court to assist with the disposition of the case. It is beyond the scope of this book to provide a guide to performing such assessments. However, *Assessing Allegations of Child Sexual Abuse* (Kuehnle, 1996), *Investigative Interviews of Children: A Guide for Helping Professionals* (Pool & Lamb, 2003), and *Jeopardy in the Courtroom: A Scientific Analysis of Children's Testimony* (Ceci, 1999) present methodologies for performing such assessments and are among the best resources available.

In these types of evaluations it is extremely important to make clear to the parties requesting such assessment that the evaluator cannot and will not offer opinions as to whether the alleged abuse actually occurred. The evaluator is in court as an expert to assist the trier of fact by providing information not readily available to the nonexpert. However, it is the responsibility of the court to take the data presented and draw conclusions. Statements of opinion by mental health professionals as to whether abuse has or has not occurred usurp the role of the court and are, in my opinion, a misuse of the professional's influence and a violation of professional ethics. It cannot be emphasized enough that this area of practice is fraught with danger to the parties, as well as ethical and liability related pitfalls for the professional. Although this area can be addressed as part of either comprehensive or issue focused forensic methodologies, it should only be attempted by those who are well trained in this aspect of forensic practice.

## SUPERVISION OF VISITATION

Courts can order supervised visitation for a wide variety of reasons. Generally, supervision is ordered when there are questions about the appropriateness of a parent's behavior toward his or her children, when there are allegations of domestic violence or substance abuse, or for any other reason that might lead the court to approach visitation conservatively. Generally, this issue is best assessed by the court or by the guardian. Mental health professionals may assist the court in determining whether the underlying problems that led to the need for supervision can be or have been addressed through treatment, medication, or other types of interventions. For example, a parent may act inappropriately during visits due to an exacerbation of a mental condition such as depression. In such a case the evaluator might interview that parent, review therapy records, and interview the current therapist, as well as observe a supervised visit. Depending on the situation, the children may also be interviewed regarding their views about visitation. Having gathered such information, the evaluator can provide the court with information about the parent's current condition and prognosis, and the advisability of allowing unsupervised visits.

## RIGHTS OF GRANDPARENTS TO VISIT

Generally, this is another area that is probably best assessed by the guardian and the court. In certain situations, the evaluator can gather information about the relationship between the grandparents and the children, evaluate the grandparents if appropriate, and possibly observe a visit between the grandparents and the children.

## INFLUENCE OF COMPANIONS OF EITHER PARTY ON THE CHILDREN

In many cases, stepparents or unmarried partners of divorced parents may play an important role in the lives of the family's children, and it may be appropriate to evaluate them regarding parenting ability, substance abuse, relationship with the children, or any other of the areas that might arise in the assessment of a natural parent. For example, there may be issues in the history of a mother's new male companion that raise questions for the court, such as a past DWI conviction. In such a situation, the evaluator may be asked to perform a drug and alcohol evaluation in order to rule out a contemporaneous substance abuse problem that could have a negative impact on the family's children. The evaluator may find that the individual quit drinking or greatly moderated his drinking after the arrest, which occurred 15 years previously when he was in his early 20s. Concerns may be raised about the father's new wife, who had founded child protective service complaints concerning her natural children from a previous marriage.

Examination of the situation by the evaluator may reveal that the previous charges related to emotional abuse of the children when the mother was in a recurrent manic state, and that she continues to have such episodes up to the present time. Finally, there may be no particular problems noted, but a guardian ad litem may want potential stepparents interviewed and given a general assessment so that all bases are covered.

## MATURITY OF CHILDREN STATING A PREFERENCE

This is an issue that can arise as a discrete referral question, or it may be raised as part of a general comprehensive assessment. New Hampshire is fairly typical in having a legal standard that specifically addresses this issue. The Butterick standard states that the court can, at its discretion, take the preferences of a "mature minor" regarding custody arrangement into account. The rule offers little in the way of guidance to the clinician as to what is meant by the term "mature minor," and as a consequence the evaluator must decide how to conceptualize such an assessment. There are several ways to approach the problem which are not mutually exclusive. The evaluator should review school records for information about the child's functioning in academic and social spheres: Teacher comments may provide information about the child's coping skills and emotional stability. Teachers may also be asked to complete a child behavior rating scale. My personal preference is to use the BASC-2, because it is comprehensive, well normed, assesses adaptive behavior as well as emotional and behavioral problems, and has parallel child/adolescent self-report, parent report, and teacher report versions. Other scales, such as the CRS-R and the PIC-2, may also be utilized in this manner. The child's parents should be interviewed regarding the child's social maturity and coping skills. Obviously, the child should be interviewed, not only to help the evaluator assess the child's apparent maturity, but also to learn the child's preferences regarding custody and the rationale for these preferences. Finally, the only commercially available test that I know for children and adolescents which has an explicit maturity scale is the Jesness Inventory-Revised. The Jesness is often used with delinquent youth, but it also has nondelinquent children and adolescents in the norming sample. The Maturity scale measures the extent to which the subject endorses beliefs and attitudes consistent with those of younger children. Utilizing some combination of test results, collateral and interview data, and clinical judgment informed by the evaluator's knowledge of child and adolescent behavior and development, it is possible to present the court or guardian ad litem with useful information to address the relative maturity of the minor. As with all components of the issue focused forensic evaluation, evaluators should "show their work" and make the basis for their conclusions explicit.

## TRAVEL ARRANGEMENTS AND TIME, PLACE, AND MANNER OF EXCHANGE FOR VISITS

Travel arrangements and pick-ups/drop-offs are often contentious issues in acrimonious divorces. I have seen many custody settlements fall apart on the issue of whether the child should be transported by one or the other parent and the location of the transfer (e.g., school, police station, rest stop halfway between the two houses). Because forensic evaluators have no more expertise in this area than any judge, guardian ad litem, or layperson with experience transporting children in cars, their input is usually not required regarding this issue. The guardian ad litem and court are presumed to be aware of the negative effects on children of the parents' bickering or worse at transfers, and of the need to induce the parents to refrain from such behavior.

## ASSESSMENT OF BOND BETWEEN CHILD AND EACH PARENT AND/OR BETWEEN SIBLINGS

In my experience, this issue generally arises in a comprehensive evaluation, but in some child custody and termination of parental rights cases, courts order a "bonding assessment." This is a contentious, controversial, and problematic issue for a number of reasons. Although it is beyond the scope of this book to review the history and research on bonding and attachment in general, as attachment theory is almost a field unto itself, we will touch on it here briefly.

A fundamental problem in assessing this area of functioning is the fact that evaluators and theorists often use different terms (bond, attachment, psychological parent) in discussing the issue, and they also have differing conceptions of what these terms mean. The concept of attachment is primarily associated with the work of John Bowlby (1969, 1973, 1980). Bowlby was one of the first experts to focus on the adverse effects of inadequate maternal care in early childhood. He saw the development of a psychological bond between the infant and the maternal caretaker as a biologically determined survival mechanism designed to maximize the infant's chances of survival. The psychological bond was seen as fundamentally different from other positive or affectionate relationships in that it is integral to the child's fundamental sense of security. According to Bowlby and later attachment theorists, children are bonded to a particular individual when they seek closeness and physical proximity to that person when they perceive serious internal or external threats to their well-being. Milchman (2000) points out that a child's perception of threats changes and develops across the life span. Early internal threats such as hunger, illness, and fatigue give way to more abstract threats to emotional equilibrium, while early perceptions of external danger such as loud noises change over time into more differentiated fears of kidnapping, gunshots, or social rejection. But regardless of the nature of the perceived threat, the child turns to the bonded caretaker for comfort and protection.

As previously discussed, Goldstein et al. offered their own view of attachment in their seminal work *Beyond the Best Interests of the Child* (1979). This work has had an enormous influence on both the law in relation to child dependency matters and on child protection and social service agencies. A central idea in this treatise is that divorce and child dependency courts should give considerable priority to protecting the relationship between a child and his or her primary attachment figure, which Goldstein and colleagues termed the psychological parent. This conceptualization of the psychological parent differs from the term "attachment" as it is generally used, in that it is more black and white; there are no degrees of intensity or multiple psychological parents. In addition, Goldstein et al. believed that there would be dire consequences if the bond between the child and the psychological parent were broken by even short interruptions or placement outside the family home. Although this interval may be extended as the child matures, Goldstein and colleagues suggest that irreparable damage can occur to children 2 years old or under in a matter of a few days of separation. Goldstein et al. also make it clear that in cases where a young child is placed with surrogate parents for periods approaching a year, these caretakers should automatically be considered the psychological parents.

This conceptualization of the parent-child attachment has been criticized over the years. A number of authors have suggested that, although there is a good deal of support for the idea of disruption of attachment being associated with adjustment problems in the child, the same kind of support does not exist for the proposition that short separations or disruptions inevitably produce severe and permanent damage. There has also been a growing recognition that children can have multiple significant psychological attachments that vary in intensity; the issue is not thought to be as dichotomous as suggested by Goldstein et al. However, the idea that a child has one psychological parent has been absorbed into the legal culture and continues to be influential in custody and placement decisions.

These conceptualizations of attachment and bonding have become important issues in divorce-related custody cases and in termination of parental rights proceedings. Unfortunately, assessment of these issues is much more abstract and difficult to quantify than other important issues that courts consider in these types of cases. Although it is relatively easy to assess a parent's concrete caretaker behaviors, qualitative aspects of the relationship between parent and child are extraordinarily subjective. However, because courts are sensitized to the potential impact of disruption of children's important psychological relationships, they commonly order "bonding assessments" of children and their caretakers. In some cases, the court has concerns about the merits of competing placements, such as a choice between a long-term, highly competent foster care provider and a less competent natural parent. In divorce-related custody assessments, the issue of bonding may arise when one parent has been the primary caretaker of the family's children, or when one of the parents has been absent. Bonding assessments can also arise in the context of allegations of parental alienation. Such assessments are likely to be complex and time-consuming, and conclusions drawn by experts can be highly subjective. Further, it is difficult to evaluate many of these assessments in terms of their reliability and scientific validity. Even more important, putting aside for the moment the question of the scientific status of attachment theory, mental health professionals commonly present opinions regarding a child's psychological relationships and attachments which are inconsistent with the assumptions of attachment theory.

It is not uncommon for bonding assessments presented to the court to consist of interviews with caretakers, a general review of case documentation, and observations of the child interacting with caretakers in the mental health professional's office. With younger children, these observations often take the form of having the adult engage the child in some type of play activity and observing the interaction between them. The mental health professional notes whether the parent's interactions with the child are appropriate, supportive, and responsive to the child's requests. However, Milchman (2000) has pointed out that the majority of professionals conducting bonding assessments base their conclusions on a fundamental error: They erroneously equate affectionate or friendly interactions with evidence of attachment. Milchman correctly points out that this is an error, because a positive interaction in a play situation is not evidence of psychological attachment. Children have many affectionate and friendly relationships; they may enjoy their association with day care teachers, coaches, or uncles, but this does not make them bonded relationships with psychological significance. As previously mentioned, attachment relationships are specifically defined as those which provide children with a sense of security when they are faced with insecurity and threat. Observations that a child plays well and enjoys contact with a caretaker in a mental health professional's office are not evidence of such attachment. Despite this, such observations are commonly presented to the court as evidence of psychological bonding.

This is not to suggest that such observations are unnecessary or cannot provide useful information. Dyer (1999) suggests that a number of procedures be used when collecting data about attachment. He recommends that bonding assessments include:

- An interview with the parents and/or caretakers of the child to provide background information and to assess the adult's attitude toward the child
- An observation of the child with the adult
- An individual interview with the child (in the case of children who are capable of meaningful verbal communication)
- A thorough review of all available information concerning the child's history

Dyer suggests that evaluators attend to certain behaviors during bonding assessments of young children, including frequency and nature of touching between child and parent, comfort-seeking behavior by the child, and the capacity of the parent to engage the child effectively and to respond to the child's expressed needs in an appropriate manner.

Other indicia of attachment include eye contact and mutual smiling, as well as the child's reaction to brief separations in the course of the conjoint interview.

Children who return to foster parents in an agitated state subsequent to brief visitation with a parent are often thought to be upset by contact with the parent, to lack close attachments with the parent, and to have negative associations with the parent. Although it may seem counterintuitive, this is often evidence of strong bonding to the biological parent. Well-bonded children do not handle visitation well, and anxiety engendered by reintroduction to and removal from the birth parent can be manifest in a variety of ways. Such children may express anger at the parents, or they may ignore them. Observations that children are calm and happy and had an apparently positive experience during a visit may, in fact, be an example of a weak or tenuous psychological bond.

All of this being said, an important caveat must be raised about the limitations of data drawn from even the best and most thorough assessments of attachment and bonding in children. Although a great deal of literature has been produced related to these issues, there is a serious disconnection between the voluminous empirical literature on the concept of attachment per se and the assessment of attachment in forensic contexts. There is a great deal of support for the proposition that children do form important psychological bonds with caretakers and that the disruption of these relationships can have a deleterious effect on development. The idea that there are different types of attachment also has empirical support. However, the reliability and validity of mental health professionals' assessments of bonding and attachment is much more tenuous. This is due in part to the nature of the issue being assessed; children cannot be systematically separated from their caretakers and allowed to develop psychopathology in order to test these hypotheses any more than children can be systematically abused to determine the psychological effects of maltreatment. As a consequence, theories about the effects of disrupted attachment on children must of necessity be observational and longitudinal.

Nevertheless, it is an open question as to whether mental health professionals' assessments of bonds and predictions about adjustment in the light of attachment would weather a *Daubert* test. The criteria for evaluating the scientific basis of expert testimony laid out in *Daubert* include:

- Whether the theory has been subjected to peer review
- The potential error rate of procedures based on the theory
- Whether standards and procedures govern assessments based on a particular theory
- The acceptance of the theory in the relevant field

A review of the relevant literature on the subject of bonding assessment shows clearly that it is highly questionable whether the assessment of attachment and bonding of children and parents as performed by mental health professionals would satisfy the requirements laid out by *Daubert*. However, the rules of evidence are not strictly applied in child custody and dependency matters, and presiding justices generally take a liberal view of the admissibility of expert testimony in these venues. Justices and marital masters utilize information elicited through cross-examination and their own judgments about what weight to give such testimony, rather than relying on strict adherence to *Daubert* and *Frye* (*Frye v. United States*, 1923) criteria. This leaves courts with the unenviable task of making sense of testimony regarding attachment and bonding when mental health professionals disagree substantially about the nature of attachment and lack a standard protocol for assessing the issue. The lack of "hard" research in this area, combined with the difficulty of applying what data exist about children in general to the specifics of the instant case, makes the issue even more difficult to sort out. This being the case, the following recommendations may prove helpful to courts dealing with these matters.

Experts who perform assessments of bonding and attachment should clearly explicate their conceptualization of these terms. It is important to know whether the expert is utilizing terms such as "attachment," "bond," and "psychological parent" in a manner consistent with the meaning suggested by the classic attachment literature, or whether he or she is utilizing the terms in a more general, nonspecific way.

Mental health experts have an affirmative ethical obligation to inform the court of limitations in their data and methodology. In terms of attachment and bonding assessments, this requires experts to clearly inform the court of the theoretical underpinnings of their conclusions. In addition, they should clearly state the relationship between the conclusions they reach about bonding and assessment in a particular case and the data they relied on in reaching these conclusions. From a practical standpoint, the court should expect experts to provide information to back up their conclusions and show a logical nexus between the data and their recommendations.

## SUMMARY

The purpose of this discussion of the issue focused forensic model of child custody assessment is not to provide an exhaustive guide to the assessment of every issue that might lend itself to this model of assessment. Rather, its purpose is to provide an overview of this approach and to help practitioners adapt this approach to their own work. That being said, I think it is important to review the main points that should be taken from this book.

1. Although I have utilized the New Hampshire Order on Appointment of the Guardian Ad Litem as the framework for this discussion of the issue focused forensic assessment, evaluators working in other jurisdictions should adapt whatever guidelines apply in their own home jurisdictions. If you live in a state where such guidelines have not been promulgated, it is advisable to utilize other guidelines, such as Schutz et al.'s (1989) list of high-consensus custody-related factors. Using these types of guidelines and lists of factors to be considered serves the purpose of structuring and orienting the evaluation.

2. It is essential to make the purpose and scope of an issue focused forensic child custody assessment explicit to all the parties (court, parents, guardian ad litem). The evaluator should clearly delineate those issues that he or she is going to assess, and it is just as important to be clear about what is not going to be addressed. For example, if the issue for the evaluator is the mental health of the parents, I include a passage such as the following in the referral section of my report:

> The purpose of this evaluation is to provide the court with information about the mental health and level of adaptation of Mr. and Mrs. Smith. Opinions will be offered as to whether either of the parties suffers from psychopathology of a type and/or intensity that could have the potential for compromising his or her

parenting ability in and of itself. In addition, this assessment will provide a description of Mr. and Mrs. Smith's overall personality styles and characteristic methods of coping with stress. This evaluation is not intended to address the issue of the best interest of the Smith children, except insofar as evidence of gross incapacity to parent emerges in the assessment, nor will any opinion be offered regarding custody and visitation. The information in this assessment must be considered in the context of all other information elicited by the guardian ad litem and the court.

3. The evaluator who uses any custody methodology should take particular care in the area of informed consent. This involves writing an explicit evaluation agreement that details the purpose of the evaluation, the techniques that will be employed, and the types of conclusions that will and will not be rendered. (See the sample agreement on pp. 61-65.) This gives the practitioner a good deal of "cover" if any of the parties complains afterward that the evaluation was not complete, ignored important data, or provided conclusions outside the scope of the evaluation.

4. In keeping with the "Ethical Principles of Psychologists and Code of Conduct" of the American Psychological Association (2002), it is incumbent on evaluators using this model to be competent to assess the issues they are addressing. Those doing issue focused forensic assessments regarding substance abuse should be familiar with the literature and have experience, supervision, and training in that area. The same applies to any of the other areas that might be the focus of an issue focused forensic evaluation. Remember, it is in the practice area of custody assessment that mental health professionals are most likely to draw an ethics complaint. If one of the parties complains that the evaluator was underqualified or inexperienced, the burden is on that practitioner to show that this is not the case.

In conclusion, I must reiterate that the issue focused forensic child custody assessment is not designed to replace the comprehensive model.

In many child custody situations, a wide-ranging assessment that explores many facets of family functioning is the appropriate way to proceed, and to do less risks a harmful disposition for the family involved. I believe that the issue focused forensic evaluation model is clearly superior to the mini-eval, which attempts to answer questions regarding the best interest of the children in a "quick and dirty" fashion, exemplifying the Melton et al. (2007) concern about egregious overreaching by custody evaluators. The issue focused forensic assessment attempts to provide in-depth information to the court about specified areas germane to the issues at hand and provides a useful alternative for the evaluation of circumscribed custody-related issues.

# **APPENDICES**

# CUSTODY EVALUATION AGREEMENT

This Agreement contains important information about my professional services and business policies. Please read it carefully, and please contact me if you have questions about any of its provisions. If you decide to proceed with this evaluation, your signature on this document will represent an Agreement between us.

## Parties to Be Evaluated
- Mother
- Father

## Specific Referral Questions to Be Addressed in the Report
- Are there any indications of gross mental illness or incapacity that would affect either parent's parenting?
- Is parental alienation present, and if so what steps are recommended to remedy the situation?
- What custody arrangements are recommended?
- What, if any, treatment or follow-up is recommended for parents and children?

**Note:** *The scope of this evaluation is limited to the specific referral questions described above. I ask that the parties not call or send me letters or emails containing information or allegations unrelated to the referral questions.*

## Areas to Be Addressed in the Report
- Mental status examination of both parents
- Brief personal history of both parents and children
- Parenting skills of both parents
- Parents' relationship with each other and with children
- Relationships between children
- Work and scheduling as they relate to custody/visitation arrangements
- General mental health and adjustment of parents and children
- Health or other physical considerations affecting parents and children
- Mental illness or incapacity affecting either parent's parenting abilities
- Both parents' general parenting style
- Presence or absence of parental alienation
- Custody/visitation preferences of children

## Sources of Information

***Note:*** *In cases involving custody and visitation issues, I ask that parents not call or send me letters or emails containing unsubstantiated allegations against the other party. Allegations by parents against one another will not be addressed in this evaluation unless they have been established as fact through objective proof. This proof would be in the form of police records, court documents, medical records, or other official documents sent to me directly by the guardian ad litem, the parties' lawyers, physicians, therapists, or other care providers. I will also consider first-hand information given to me by professionals involved in the case. Only information that relates directly to the referral question(s) will be considered.*

- **Interviews (to be conducted in my office):**
  Mother alone–approximately 1 hour
  Mother with child(ren)–approximately 1 hour
  Father alone–approximately 1 hour
  Father with child(ren)–approximately 1 hour
  Each child alone–approximately 30 to 40 minutes with each child
- **Testing:**
  Mother
      MMPI-2
  Father
      MMPI-2
- **Collateral Sources of Information:**
  Guardian ad litem
  Mother's lawyer
  Father's lawyer
  Physicians, therapists, or other care providers, if relevant
  Other parties directly involved in this case, if relevant
- **Records:**
  Court documents
  Medical records
  Police records

***Note:*** *Any documents provided should be sent to me directly by the guardian ad litem, the parties' lawyers, physicians, therapists, or other care providers.*

## Releases

I will need the following releases from the parties:

- **Mother**
  - Guardian ad litem
  - Mother's lawyer
  - Father's lawyer
  - Physicians, therapists, or other care providers, if relevant
  - Other parties directly involved in this case, if relevant
- **Father**
  - Guardian ad litem
  - Father's lawyer
  - Mother's lawyer
  - Physicians, therapists, or other care providers, if relevant
  - Other parties directly involved in this case, if relevant

## Evaluator's Role

If the parties decide to proceed, I will be conducting an independent custody evaluation. I will not be advocating for or providing treatment to any of the parties involved, and will not be able to provide follow-up treatment once the evaluation is complete.

## Professional Fees

The cost of this evaluation will be $_____, to be divided equally between the two parties and to be paid in advance. This fee will include all necessary interviews, collateral contacts, record review, test administration, scoring and interpretation, and a written report.

Once the evaluation is complete, I will be available for depositions, court appearances, or to meet with the parties or speak to them by telephone at my applicable hourly rate, to be paid by the party requesting the service. If future services are anticipated by either party, a retainer may be requested to serve as a credit balance against which fees are charged. Any unused portion of the retainer will be returned to the payer promptly when I receive notice that no further services are needed. My fees and billing policies are detailed in the enclosed "Office Policies and Billing Information" sheet.

## Confidentiality

Within certain limits, client information is kept strictly confidential and is not revealed to anyone without written permission. However, the parties should be aware of the following exceptions:

- To gain the benefit of a second opinion I may occasionally consult other health and mental health professionals about a case, with care being taken to protect my clients' privacy and identity. The other professionals are also legally bound to keep the information confidential.
- It is necessary to share certain protected client information with staff for administrative and clerical purposes, such as scheduling, billing, and report preparation. All staff are given training about protecting my clients' privacy and must agree not to release any information outside of the practice without the permission of a professional staff member.
- In addition, under the circumstances described below I am required by law to reveal confidential information to other persons or agencies without a client's permission.

1. If a patient communicates a serious threat of physical violence against a clearly identified or reasonably identifiable victim or victims, or a serious threat of substantial damage to real property, I may be required to take protective actions. These actions may include notifying the potential victim, contacting the police, or seeking involuntary hospitalization for the patient.
2. If there is an indication of a clear and present danger of self-harm, I may be obligated to inform family members, agencies, or others who might help to protect the client's safety.
3. If a court of law issues a legitimate subpoena, I must provide the information described in the subpoena.
4. If a client is in therapy or being tested by order of a court of law, information may be revealed to the court.
5. If I have reason to suspect that a child has been abused or neglected, the law requires that I file a report with the Bureau of Child and Family Services. Once such a report is filed, I may be required to provide additional information.
6. If I suspect or have a good faith reason to believe that any incapacitated adult has been subjected to abuse, neglect, self-neglect, or exploitation, or is living in hazardous conditions, the law requires that I file a report with the appropriate governmental agency, usually the Department of Health and Human Services. Once such a report is filed, I may be required to provide additional information.
7. If a government agency is requesting information for health oversight activities, I may be required to provide it.
8. If a patient files a complaint or lawsuit against me, I may disclose relevant information regarding that patient in order to defend myself.

**Record Requests**

The report on this psychological evaluation will be a joint report and will include confidential information concerning both parents and their children. Upon completion the report will be provided to the guardian ad litem in the case and to both parents' attorneys. The parties should contact their attorneys in order to obtain a copy of the report. If copies of the report are requested by either party in the future or by their agents, I will need signed releases from both parents in order to provide the reports.

Your signature below indicates that you have read the information in this document and agree to abide by its terms.

_____

CLIENT NAME (Please Print)

_____     _____

CLIENT SIGNATURE                         DATE

# ERIC G. MART, PH.D., ABPP

NEW HAMPSHIRE & MASSACHUSETTS LICENSED PSYCHOLOGIST
BOARD CERTIFIED FORENSIC PSYCHOLOGIST

HIGHLAND PSYCHOLOGICAL SERVICES, 311 HIGHLANDER WAY, MANCHESTER, NH 03103-7414
TEL.: (603) 626-0966 • FAX: (603) 622-7012
BOSTON OFFICE: LEWIS WHARF – BAY 232, BOSTON, MA 02110-3927 • TEL.: (617) 227-6868
WWW.PSYCHOLOGY-LAW.COM • EMART@PSYCHOLOGY-LAW.COM

## CONFIDENTIAL PSYCHOLOGICAL REPORT
### July 18, 2007

Name:   Fred Litigant
DOB:    11/10/1960
DOE:    3/12/2006
Age:    46
Gender: Male

### Reason for Referral

Mr. Litigant is currently involved in a visitation dispute with his ex-wife involving their son, Ben, who is 7 years old. Mr. Litigant's ex-wife has informed the court that Mr. Litigant was treated for depression during the course of their marriage and she is concerned that his condition could reoccur and that this would have a negative effect on his ability to properly parent Ben during visits. A psychological evaluation of Mr. Litigant has been requested to assist the guardian ad litem and the Court in resolving this matter. Specifically, the Court requests information regarding whether Mr. Litigant currently suffers from any psychological problems that are likely to compromise his ability to care for his son during visits.

It should be noted that this assessment was not designed to be a comprehensive custody evaluation. The purpose of this evaluation is to provide general information about Mr. Litigant's mental health and general level of adaptation. As a consequence, no recommendations will be made about visitation arrangements.

### Clinical Interview

Mr. Litigant was seen on a voluntary basis at my office. I discussed with Mr. Litigant issues related to confidentiality and the purpose of the evaluation. Mr. Litigant appeared to understand these issues and was willing to proceed with the evaluation.

I spoke to Mr. Litigant about his personal history. He was born in Ohio and raised by both parents. He has one older brother. His family relocated several times, moving from Akron, Ohio, to Pittsburg, Pennsylvania, and finally settling in Rochester, New York, where he attended high school. His family life while growing up was "normal, happy," despite some problems in his parents' relationship. After he graduated from high school he went directly to college, where he studied liberal arts and literature. He graduated with a B.A. in English literature. Mr. Litigant subsequently attended graduate school in New York City and obtained a master's degree in English literature. He took a position at a community college in Ohio, where he taught English.

Mr. Litigant told me he was married for the first time in 1992 to a woman who also taught at the community college where he was employed. The marriage lasted for 1 year and then broke up. According to Mr. Litigant, this breakup was caused in part by his wife's difficulty with the long hours he put into his job. He told me that he and his wife attempted to deal with their problems in marriage counseling, but ultimately decided to divorce. He met Alice Litigant through a mutual friend and they were married in 1998. Ms. Litigant was attending college to become a teacher. After she graduated they moved to New Hampshire, where Ms. Litigant now works as a special educator. Mr. Litigant feels that their relationship was always difficult. He reports that his wife could be very moody. He also reports that after their son, Ben, was born his wife became extremely focused on the baby, and he felt shut out as a parent. It was during this period of time that he became depressed. He sought treatment from Dr. Jones, who is a psychiatrist. He reports that he was diagnosed with dysthymia and was treated with Wellbutrin, which he found helpful. Mr. Litigant eventually moved out of the house, and in the divorce proceedings that followed he asked for joint physical custody. At the present time his ex-wife has primary physical custody of Ben. Mr. Litigant moved to Montpelier, Vermont, 3 years ago, and now sees his son for one extended weekend a month and splits custodial time during holidays and school vacations. He also has two separate 2-week periods of visitation in the summer.

Mr. Litigant told me that the issue of his past treatment for depression had not been an issue until recently, when he and his ex-wife had a disagreement about scheduling visits, and he went back to court to obtain more custodial time. He told me that he stopped seeing Dr. Jones 10 months ago and that he had tapered off his medication under the doctor's supervision at that time. He said that he can go back to Dr. Jones if he develops further depressive symptoms, but that this has not been necessary since the divorce was finalized. Mr. Litigant told me that he enjoys his time with his son, and that the visits go well.

## Assessment Procedures

Therapist Interview  
Guardian Ad Litem Interview  
Clinical Interview  
Mental Status Checklist for Adults  
Adult-Adolescent Parenting Inventory-2  
Minnesota Multiphasic Personality Inventory-2  
Logical Rorschach

## Interview With Guardian Ad Litem

With Mr. Litigant's permission, I spoke to Attorney Joan Smith, who is the guardian ad litem in this case. Ms. Smith told me that she has been involved in this case for over 1 year and has extensive knowledge of the case and participants. She has observed Ben with both parents and has also been to both family homes. Ms. Smith told me that based on all of the information she has, there are no indications that either parent has any difficulty in his or her relations with Ben, whom she sees as a normal 7 year old who has adjusted well to his parent's divorce. She has noticed that Ben becomes stressed when his parents disagree, and sometimes feels he is caught in a loyalty bind, but this is not too much of a problem. She has seen no signs that Mr. Litigant has any difficulties parenting Ben due to depression or for any other reason. She has spoken to Ben and he told her he enjoys going to his father's home for visits, but that the ride is long and he sometimes misses his friends.

## Interview With Dr. Jones

After having obtained a release from Mr. Litigant, I spoke to Dr. Jones, who is the psychiatrist who treated Mr. Litigant. Dr. Jones told me that he saw Mr. Litigant as someone with pre-existing depressive tendencies that were exacerbated by the pressures of his divorce. He described Mr. Litigant as having presented with moderate symptoms of dysthymia that did not have a serious impact on his ability to perform activities of daily living, nor did it affect his social and occupational roles, aside from minor problems. Significantly, Dr. Jones made it clear that Mr. Litigant had never voiced any thoughts of self-harm or harm to others, and there was never any significant interference in his thought patterns. Dr. Jones indicated that Mr. Litigant responded well to Wellbutrin, and after his situation stabilized he tapered off of the medication without difficulty. The doctor confirmed that Mr. Litigant is free to come back for additional consultation on an as-needed basis. Dr. Jones also noted that he never thought that Mr. Litigant's depression was severe enough to have a serious impact on his parenting abilities.

## Results of Testing

### *Mental Status Checklist for Adults*

Presenting Problem

Mr. Litigant's major presenting problem was reported as being a visitation issue.

Physical and Behavioral Description

Mr. Litigant is a 46-year-old white male who appeared to be his stated age. He is of average height and weight. His eye color is hazel and his hair is brown. Mr. Litigant's manner of dress was appropriate to the office setting and his hygiene appeared to be good. In completing the interview he required the use of glasses. Mr. Litigant's gait was normal. His posture was normal. Motor behavior during the interview was unremarkable.

During the interview Mr. Litigant was alert. His level of responsiveness did not show obvious effects of pain, medications, or drugs. There were no overt signs of distress during the interview. Mr. Litigant's facial expression was appropriate to the content of the interview topic. Eye contact during the interview was appropriately focused. Speech quantity, both spontaneously and in response to questions, was normal. Speech quality was normal. There was no suggestion of a foreign or strong regional accent, stuttering, articulation problems, or mimicking of the examiner's speech.

Emotional Status

Mr. Litigant's mood was calm and cheerful. His affect, or emotional responsiveness, was appropriate to the content of discussion. Mr. Litigant denied current feelings of depression and indicated that he has not experienced any episodes of depression in the past 6 months. Common symptoms of depression, including loss of appetite, guilt, motor retardation, sleep disturbance, fatigue, weight loss, and decreased sexual interest, were all denied. No signs of anxiety were observed during the interview. Mr. Litigant denied any current feelings of anxiety and any episodes of anxiety in the previous 6 months. Common symptoms of anxiety, including shortness of breath, palpitations, chest pain, dizziness, faintness, excessive sweating, paresthesias, muscle aches, cold hands, gastrointestinal problems, muscle twitching, and dry mouth, were all denied.

Mr. Litigant's thought processes were logical and coherent. Content of thought was unremarkable and appropriate to the purposes of the interview. There were no indications of the presence of delusions. Mr. Litigant denied problems with common compulsions. He has not been bothered by obsessive thoughts. His daily life is not significantly affected by common phobias. Auditory, visual, and olfactory hallucinations were denied. Mr. Litigant has no recent history of loss of consciousness, seizures, or black-outs.

Evaluation of cognitive processes indicated that Mr. Litigant's attention and concentration skills were normal. He was oriented for person, place, and time. Immediate, recent, and remote memory were intact. No amnesia was reported. There was no evidence of unconscious fabrication of responses, as sometimes occurs with memory disorders. Mr. Litigant's intellectual ability was estimated as being in the superior range. There was no indication of notable decline of intellectual ability. Mr. Litigant's fund of information was consistent with his background and intellectual level. Abstracting ability appeared to be normal. Computational skills were judged to be within normal limits. Evaluation of language skills revealed no evidence of aphasia. There was no obvious evidence of other cognitive deficits typically associated with brain dysfunction.

Health and Habits

Review of Mr. Litigant's medical status revealed that he has had treatment for reflux. Mr. Litigant reported concerns about pain related to past athletic injuries. He is a nonsmoker with no history of cigarette smoking. Use of alcohol was reported to be occasional and use of illicit drugs was denied. He reported no history of alcohol or drug abuse. Mr. Litigant reported that his weight has remained stable. His appetite has remained unchanged. Mr. Litigant has experienced no recent changes to his sleep pattern. He is interested in sexual relations, but is not currently active. The level of his sexual interest has not changed recently. Mr. Litigant's sexual orientation is exclusively heterosexual.

Legal Issues/Aggressive Behavior

Mr. Litigant denied any history of suicide attempts or violent acts towards others, including family members. Current thoughts of self-injury or violence to others were denied. His demeanor during the interview gave no indication of aggressive or violent behavior.

Current Living Situation

Review of Mr. Litigant's current living situation reveals that he is presently employed as a college professor. Review of Mr. Litigant's educational background established that he has both college and postgraduate degrees. He is presently divorced from his second wife and lives alone in an apartment. He has one natural offspring; no children presently live with him.

## Adult-Adolescent Parenting Inventory-2

The Adult-Adolescent Parenting Inventory-2 is an objective test designed to assist in the assessment of parenting and child rearing attitudes of adolescent and adult populations. It was developed from the known parenting and child rearing practices of abusive and neglectful parents, and provides an index of risk for child abuse.

The AAPI-2 has five clinical scales. These are Inappropriate Expectations of Children, Inability to Be Empathically Aware of Children's Needs, Strong Belief in the Value and Use of Corporal Punishment, Parent-Child Role Reversal, and Oppressing Children's Power and Independence.

Mr. Litigant's scores were in the average range on all five scales of the AAPI compared to nonabusive parents. This indicates that he can articulate appropriate answers to questions about parenting techniques and attitudes. However, it may not accurately reflect his behavior with child, and does not guarantee that he will put his knowledge of parenting into action in an appropriate manner.

## Minnesota Multiphasic Personality Inventory-2

The MMPI-2 is an objective personality inventory with 3 validity scales, 10 clinical scales, and a number of content and research scales.

Mr. Litigant's scores on the validity scales of the MMPI-2 were within normal limits. This indicates that he approached the instrument in a straightforward and reliable manner and that the results most likely represent an accurate picture of his present personality functioning.

Mr. Litigant had no clinical elevations on his MMPI-2 protocol. He had several transitional level scores which are suggestive of certain personality issues that may have a bearing on this case. There are indications that he is prone to worry and has difficulty making decisions when under stress. He tends to be pessimistic about the future and may withdraw from others when under stress. At the same time, he is likely to be a motivated therapy patient and is likely to have a positive response to psychotherapeutic intervention.

## Summary and Conclusions

The results of this evaluation indicate that Mr. Litigant is a reasonably well-adjusted individual who is free from significant psychopathology. It is clear from Mr. Litigant's self-report, the results of this assessment, and my conversations with his psychiatrist and the guardian ad litem, that he has a history of mild to moderate dysthymia, but that it was easily treated. He appears never to have developed major depression, and there is no evidence that his symptoms ever had any significant impact on his ability to meet the demands of his social or occupational roles or his ability to parent his son during visits. The guardian ad litem's home visit, observations of father and son, and interviews with Ben, support the conclusion that Mr. Litigant's past depressive symptoms did not create any problems regarding visitation in the past, and there are no indications of current problems in this respect. Based on this information, it is my opinion that Mr. Litigant does not currently suffer from any form of psychological maladjustment that would be likely, in and of itself, to create significant deficits in his parenting ability. As mentioned at the outset of this report, the guardian and the court will wish to consider this opinion in the context of the totality of the information available.

*Eric Mart, Ph. D.*

Eric G. Mart, Ph.D., ABPP (Forensic)

EGM / km

74

# REFERENCES

Ackerman, M. J., & Ackerman, M. C. (1997). Custody evaluation practices: A 1996 survey of experienced professionals (revisited). *Professional Psychology: Research and Practice, 28*(2), 137-145.

American Psychiatric Association. (2000). *Diagnostic and Statistical Manual for Mental Disorders* (*DSM-IV-TR*; 4th ed. text rev.). Washington, DC: Author.

American Psychological Association. (1994). Guidelines for child custody evaluations in divorce proceedings. *American Psychologist, 49*, 677-680.

American Psychological Association. (2002). Ethical principles of psychologists and code of conduct. *American Psychologist, 57*, 1060-1073.

Amundson, J. K., Daya, R., & Gill, E. (2000). A minimalist approach to child custody evaluation. *American Journal of Forensic Psychology, 18*(3), 63-87.

Association of Family and Conciliation Courts. (2006). *AFCC Model Standards of Practice for Child Custody Evaluation*. Madison, WI: Author (www.afccnet.org).

Bavolek, S. J., & Keene, R. G. (1999). *Adult-Adolescent Parenting Inventory-2 (AAPI-2) Manual*. Schaumburg, IL: Family Development Resources.

Bowlby, J. (1969). *Attachment and Loss* (Vol. 1). New York: Basic Books.

Bowlby, J. (1973). *Separation: Anxiety and Anger. Attachment and Loss* (Vol. 2). New York: Basic Books.

Bowlby, J. (1980). *Loss: Sadness and Depression. Attachment and Loss* (Vol. 3). New York: Basic Books.

Butcher, J. N., Graham, J. R., Ben-Porath, Y. S., Tellegen, A., Dahlstrom, W. G., & Kaemmer, B. (2001). *Minnesota Multiphasic Personality Inventory-2 (MMPI-2) Manual for Administration, Scoring, and Interpretation* (rev. ed.). Minneapolis: University of Minnesota Press.

Butcher, J. N., Williams, C. L., Graham, J. R., Archer, R. P., Tellegen, A., Ben-Porath, Y. S., & Kaemmer, B. (2001). *Minnesota Multiphasic Personality Inventory-Adolescent (MMPI-A) Manual for Administration, Scoring, and Interpretation.* Minneapolis, MN: University of Minnesota Press.

Ceci, S. J. (1999). *Jeopardy in the Courtroom: A Scientific Analysis of Children's Testimony.* Washington, DC: American Psychological Association.

Committee on Ethical Guidelines for Forensic Psychologists. (1991). Specialty guidelines for forensic psychologists. *Law and Human Behavior, 15*(6), 655-665.

Conners, C. K. (1997). *Conners' Rating Scales-Revised (CRS-R) Manual.* Toronto, Ontario, Canada: Multi-Health Systems.

*Daubert v. Merrell Dow Pharmaceuticals, Inc.,* 509 U.S. 579 (1993).

Dawes, R. M., Faust, D., & Meehl, P. E. (1989). Clinical versus actuarial judgement. *Science, 243*(4899), 1668-1674.

DeClue, G. (2002). The best interests of the village children. *Journal of Psychiatry and Law, 30*(3), 355-390.

Dougherty, E. H., & Schinka, J. A. (1989). *Developmental History Checklist for Children.* Lutz, FL: Psychological Assessment Resources.

*Dusky v. United States,* 362 U.S. 402 (1960).

Dyer, F. J. ( 1999). *Psychological Consultation in Parental Rights Cases.* New York: Guilford.

Everington, E. T. (1992) *Competence Assessment for Standing Trial for Defendants With Mental Retardation: CAST-MR Test Manual.* Worthington, OH: International Diagnostic Services.

Exner, J. E. (2003). *The Rorschach: A Comprehensive System* (4th ed.). New York: John Wiley.

*Frye v. United States,* 293 F. 1013 (D.C. Cir. 1923).

Garb, H. N. (1998). *Studying the Clinician: Judgment Research and Psychological Assessment.* Washington, DC: American Psychological Association.

Goldstein, J. A., Freud, A., & Solnit, A. J. (1979). *Beyond the Best Interests of the Child*. New York: Free Press.

Gould, J. W. (2006). *Conducting Scientifically Crafted Child Custody Evaluations* (2nd ed.). Sarasota, FL: Professional Resource Press.

Grisso, T. (2003). *Evaluating Competencies: Forensic Assessments and Instruments* (2nd ed.). New York: Kluwer Academic/Plenum.

Heinze, M. C., & Grisso, T. (1996). Review of instruments assessing parenting competencies used in child custody evaluations. *Behavioral Sciences and the Law, 14*(3), 293-313.

Hoge, S. K., Bonnie, R. J., Poythress, N., & Monahan, J. (1999). *The MacArthur Competence Assessment Tool-Criminal Adjudication (MacCAT-CA) Manual*. Lutz, FL: Psychological Assessment Resources.

Jesness, C. F. (1996). *Jesness Inventory-Revised (JI-R) Manual*. Toronto, Ontario, Canada: Multi-Health Systems.

Kaufman, A. S., & Kaufman, N. L. (2004). *Kaufman Brief Intelligence Test (KBIT-2) Manual* (2nd ed.). Bloomington, MN: Pearson Assessments.

Kuehnle, K. (1996). *Allegations of Child Sexual Abuse*. Sarasota, FL: Professional Resource Press.

Laboratory of Community Psychiatry, Harvard Medical School. (1973). *Competency to Stand Trial and Mental Illness* (DHEW Publication No. AMD 77-103). Rockville, MD: National Institute of Mental Health.

McGrew, K. S., & Woodcock, R. W. (2001). *Technical Manual. Woodcock-Johnson III*. Itasca, IL: Riverside.

Melton, G. B., Petrila, J., Poythress, N. G., & Slobogin, C. (2007). *Psychological Evaluations for the Courts: A Handbook for Mental Health Professionals and Lawyers* (3rd ed.). New York: Guilford.

Milchman, M. S. (2000). Mental health experts' common error in assessing bonding in guardianship cases. *Journal of Psychiatry and Law, 28*(3), 351-378.

Miller, F., Roberts, J., Brooks, M., & Lazowski, L. (1997). *SASSI-3 Users Guide: A Quick Reference for Administration and Scoring*. Bloomington, IN: The SASSI Institute.

Millon, T. (1993). *Millon Adolescent Clinical Inventory (MACI) Manual*. Minneapolis, MN: Pearson Assessments.

Millon, T., David, R. D., & Millon, C. (1997). *Millon Clinical Multiaxial Inventory-III (MCMI-III) Manual* (2nd ed.). Minneapolis, MN: Pearson Assessments.

Milner, J. S. (1986). *Child Abuse Potential Inventory (CAPI) Manual.* DeKalb, IL: Psytec, Inc.

Morey, L. C. (1991). *Personality Assessment Inventory (PAI) Professional Manual.* Lutz, FL: Psychological Assessment Resources.

Mortimer, R. G., Filkins, L. D., Lower, J. S., Kerlan, M. W., Post, D. V., Mudge, B., & Rosenblatt, C. (1971). *Court Procedures for Identifying Problem Drinkers: Report on Phase I.* Washington, DC: U.S. Department of Transportation. (DOT HS-800 630)

Munsinger, H., & Karlson, K. (1994). *Uniform Child Custody Evaluation System Manual (UCCES).* Lutz, FL: Psychological Assessment Resources.

Nochajski, T. H., & Miller, B. A. (1995). *Training Manual for the Research Institute on Addictions Self Inventory (RIASI).* Buffalo, NY: Research Institute on Addictions.

O'Donohue, W., & Bradley, A. R. (1999). Commentary. Conceptual and empirical issues in child custody evaluations. *Clinical Psychology: Science and Practice, 6*(3), 310-322.

Pool, D. A., & Lamb, M. E. (2003). *Investigative Interviews of Children: A Guide for Helping Professionals.* Washington, DC: American Psychological Association.

Popper, K. (1992). *Realism and the Aim of Science: Postscript to the Logic of Scientific Discovery.* London: Routledge.

Reynolds, C. R., & Kamphaus, R. W. (2003). *Reynolds Intellectual Assessment Scales (RIAS) Manual.* Lutz, FL: Psychological Assessment Resources.

Reynolds, C. R., & Kamphaus, R. W. (2004). *Behavior Assessment System for Children (BASC-2) Manual* (2nd ed.). Circle Pines, MN: AGS Publishing.

Rogers, R. (1995). *Diagnostic and Structured Interviewing: A Handbook for Psychologists.* Lutz, FL: Professional Assessment Resources.

Sattler, J. M. (1998). *Clinical and Forensic Interviewing of Children and Families: Guidelines for the Mental Health, Education, Pediatric, and Child Maltreatment Fields.* La Mesa, CA: Author.

Schutz, B. M., Dixon, E. B., Lindenberger, J. C., & Ruther, N. J. (1989). *Solomon's Sword: A Practical Guide to Conducting Child Custody Evaluations.* San Francisco: Jossey-Bass.

Selzer, M. (1971). The Michigan Alcohol Screening Test (MAST): The quest for a new diagnostic instrument. *American Journal of Psychiatry, 127*, 1653-1658.

Shinka, J. (1989). *Personal History Checklist for Adults (PHC)*. Lutz, FL: Psychological Assessment Resources.

Wechsler, D. (1998). *Wechsler Adult Intelligence Scale-Third Edition (WAIS-III) Manual*. San Antonio, TX: The Psychological Corporation.

Wechsler, D. (1999). *Wechsler Abbreviated Scale of Intelligence (WASI) Manual*. San Antonio, TX: The Psychological Corporation.

Wechsler, D. (2002). *Wechsler Individual Achievement Test (WIAT-II) Manual* (2nd ed.). San Antonio, TX: The Psychological Corporation.

Wechsler, D. (2003). *Wechsler Intelligence Scale for Children-Fourth Edition (WISC-IV) Manual*. San Antonio, TX: The Psychological Corporation.

Weller, E. B, Weller, R. A., Rooney, M. T., & Fristad, M. A. (1999). *Children's Interview for Psychiatric Syndromes (ChIPS) Manual*. Arlington, VA: American Psychiatric Press.

Wildman, R. W., II., Batchhelor, E. S., Thompson, L., Nelson, F. R., Moore, J. T., Patterson, M. E., et al. (1978). *The Georgia Court Competency Test (GCCT): An Attempt to Develop a Rapid, Quantitative Measure of Fitness for Trial*. Unpublished manuscript, Forensic Services Division, Central State Hospital, Milledgeville, GA.

Wilkinson, G. S., & Robertson, G. J. (2005). *Wide Range Achievement Test 4 (WRAT-4)*. Lutz, FL: Psychological Assessment Resources.

Wirt, R. D., Lachar, D., Klinedinst, J. E., Seat, P. D., & Broen, W. E. (2001). *Personality Inventory for Children (PIC-2) Manual* (2nd ed.). Los Angeles, CA: Western Psychological Services.

# If You Found This Book Useful . . .

You might want to know more about our other titles.

If you would like to receive our latest catalog, please return this form:

Name: _____
**(Please Print)**

Address: _____

Address: _____

City/State/Zip: _____
This is ☐ home   ☐ office

Telephone: (_____) _____

E-mail: _____

Fax: (_____) _____

I am a:

☐  Psychologist
☐  Psychiatrist
☐  Attorney
☐  Clinical Social Worker

☐  Mental Health Counselor
☐  Marriage and Family Therapist
☐  Not in Mental Health Field
☐  Other: _____

◆     ◆     ◆

**Professional Resource Press**
**P.O. Box 15560**
**Sarasota, FL  34277-1560**

**Telephone: 800-443-3364**
**FAX:  941-343-9201**
**E-mail: orders@prpress.com**
**Website: http://www.prpress.com**

# Add A Colleague To Our Mailing List . . .

If you would like us to send our latest catalog to one of your colleagues, please return this form:

Name: _____
(Please Print)

Address: _____

Address: _____

City/State/Zip: _____
This is  ❐ home  ❐ office

Telephone: (_____)_____

E-mail: _____

Fax: (_____) _____

This person is a:

❐  Psychologist                  ❐  Mental Health Counselor
❐  Psychiatrist                   ❐  Marriage and Family Therapist
❐  Attorney                       ❐  Not in Mental Health Field
❐  Clinical Social Worker         ❐  Other: _____

Name of person completing this form: _____

◆    ◆    ◆

**Professional Resource Press**
**P.O. Box 15560**
**Sarasota, FL  34277-1560**

**Telephone: 800-443-3364**
**FAX:  941-343-9201**
**E-mail: orders@prpress.com**
**Website: http://www.prpress.com**